What Does It Mean To Me?

A workbook explaining self awareness and
life lessons to the child or youth with
High Functioning Autism or Aspergers.

Structured teaching ideas for home and school

by Catherine Faherty

with a foreword by Dr. Gary Mesibov
Director–Division TEACCH, University of North Carolina

Future Horizons, Inc.
721 W. Abram Street
Arlington, TX 76013

800-489-0727; 817-277-0727
817-277-2270 Fax

Website: www.FutureHorizons-autism.com
E-mail: edfuture@onramp.net

ISBN #1-885477-59-7

Dedicated to my inspiration for this book:

The Asheville TEACCH Center Support Group for Parents
of high functioning children with autism
and
The Asheville TEACCH Center Social Group for Adults
with high functioning autism and Asperger Syndrome

And to my foundation:

John Faherty,
Nicholas Faherty,
Ismene Collins and Nicholas Collins

*"We should acknowledge differences,
we should greet differences,
until difference makes no difference anymore."*

—Adela A. Allen

Table of Contents

Chapter 3: The Sensory Experience 51

Chapter 4: Artistic Talent 69

Chapter 5: People 81

Chapter 6: Understanding 101

Chapter 7: Thoughts 121

Chapter 8: Communication 131

Chapter 9: School 165

Chapter 10: Friends 215

Chapter 11: Feeling Upset 243

Chapter 12: The Last Chapter 271

Forward

It is a personal thrill to introduce this marvelous book by Catherine Faherty. Catherine is a superb professional whom I have admired and enjoyed for many years. Thoughtful, creative, intelligent, and extremely committed, people with autism and their families have benefitted from her innovative approaches ever since she started working as a professional in the field of autism years ago.

Given Catherine's rich and prolific intervention strategies, I was delighted when she first told me of her plan to take a leave of absence from the TEACCH program to write this volume. Catherine seemed to be the ideal person to develop a memorable product if given the time to organize and integrate her fluent and innovative ideas. This book has exceeded my high expectations and will be an invaluable addition to the libraries of people with autism, their families, and the professionals who serve them.

The book has captured the magic that is Catherine, and that has made her such a valuable member of our TEACCH staff. It is primarily solid, informative, and very autism-friendly. Her marvelous ability to understand the perspectives of people with autism and her wonderful talent of explaining difficult concepts at a level they can understand is very special. The book deals with everyday problems and some very difficult and intimate situations and conflicts. Like Catherine, the book meets all of these challenges head-on and effectively. Parents and people with autism will be grateful for this. Catherine's warmth and genuine affection for people with autism will make her readers smile. Her practical, common sense approach makes the book readable and the activities easy to follow.

Of course, the best part of the book is the way it involves people with autism. As a teacher and therapist in the TEACCH program, Catherine always has had an uncanny knack for engaging her clients, no matter how aloof or out-of-touch they might be. This same knack is evident on every page of her book where people with autism are asked to think, react, and write down their personal thoughts. They are led step-by-step through this process, and will undoubtedly learn a great deal from their involvement. Those of us who help them through the process will learn a great deal as well.

I have thoroughly enjoyed the drafts of this book that I have reviewed and am excited that the final product is now available. I know you will enjoy and appreciate this book as much as hundreds of families have appreciated the many creative and innovative ideas that Catherine has shared with them over the years. This is a unique opportunity to help people with autism in a slightly different way. Thanks to you, Catherine, for another major contribution in a career that has produced so many of them.

Gary B. Mesibov
Professor and Director
Division TEACCH
The University of North Carolina at Chapel Hill

To the Adult Readers:
families, teachers, and friends...

*"**This** is information that every kid with autism needs to have!"*

—Thomas Johnson,
10 year old boy with high functioning autism,
after seeing the workbook

Why this book came to be

As a therapist at one of regional TEACCH Centers in North Carolina, I am often asked by parents of children with high functioning autism for information they can read about the diagnosis. It has become easier in recent years to refer them to the growing number of books and articles.

Once in a while, parents ask if there is anything their *child* can read to help him or her understand the diagnosis. This new book is an in-depth aid to help your child or student learn about autism and to help you talk together about autism's profound effects. Although this book certainly does not claim to describe every child with this diagnosis, nor does it cover all the issues, it can be a starting place for self- discovery, growth, and positive action.

Each of us, whether we have autism or not, has our own inner timetable prompting us toward greater self-knowledge. For some it begins in childhood. For many it begins in adolescence. And for others, self-awareness may not begin until adulthood. It is hoped that this book will help you support your young person with high functioning autism or Asperger Syndrome in his or her journey of self-understanding.

Use this book as a resource to educate the important people in your child's life about autism and how it might be affecting personal development, behavior, relationships, and view of the world. Share this book with those who care about your child, including the people who partner with you in developing his or her educational program.

Ultimately, it is my hope that this book will ease your child's journey.

Catherine Faherty
February 2000

Become familiar with how this book is organized

Take a few moments to look at the **Table of Contents**. You will see that there are twelve chapters. Chapter 1 introduces the term *autism* and explains the ways that you and your child will be writing in the workbook. The subsequent chapters each focus on an important aspect of life (*i.e., Communication or Understanding or Friends, etc.*).

Each chapter is divided into two parts, *Workbook* pages and a section *For Parents and Teachers*. Individual topics are listed by page number for easy reference in the Table of Contents.

Prior to beginning the book with your child, preview Chapter 1.

 ## The workbook

The workbook pages are for you and your child to read together and fill in, mark, or circle the relevant information. Suggestions for parents about this process are included in Chapter 1 on pages 15-19. The workbook pages are easily found by their dark labels on the outer edge of each workbook page.

 The workbook attempts to describe ordinary circumstances of everyday life, pointing out typical behaviors of children with autism and their neurotypical peers. It suggests in simple terms how and why the reader's experience may sometimes differ from others' experiences. With the help of a parent, teacher, or friend, the young reader is encouraged to add personal details, individualizing the information on the pages. In this way, the workbook will come to more accurately represent each child's uniqueness.

On some of the workbook pages, the young reader may be introduced to ideas or strategies that require their parents' or teachers' cooperation. *The workbook is for parents and teachers, too!* In most cases, further details about the suggestions are provided in the corresponding sections for parents and teachers in the second part of each chapter.

📖 For Parents and Teachers

The second part of each chapter is primarily for parents and teachers (and other significant adults.) This part supplements the workbook pages with related concepts, ideas, and practical suggestions for home and school.

Most of the ideas are examples of widely used TEACCH Structured Teaching strategies that this author and the other therapists, teachers, directors, and parents in the TEACCH program have developed and adapted for individual children and adults during the course of the program's existence. Other ideas are the inspired work of prominent colleagues in the field of autism, while the author's own creativity and experience are woven throughout.

For ease in reading, and to fairly represent girls and boys, three sections have been written using feminine pronouns (she and her), and nine have been written using masculine pronouns (he and his). This ratio loosely corresponds to the ratio off females to males diagnosed with autism.

Who wrote the workbook, anyway?

In the text of the workbook pages, you will notice frequent use of the first-person pronoun *"I."* My intent is not to pretend that the author is a child with autism. In fact, in earlier versions, I wrote the workbook pages in a typical manner. I wrote to the reader using second-person pronouns *"you"* and *"your"* where appropriate. However, several children and adults with autism said that when they read the word *"you,"* they weren't sure if it meant *them,* or if it meant *someone else (the literal "you")!* Consequently, I made the decision to write in the first-person, using *"I"* instead of the second-person pronoun *"you."*

My intent in writing from the first-person point of view is to provide clarity for the reader with autism, not to imply or pretend that it was written by a child with autism.

Keys to keep in mind when trying the ideas in this book

The first step is to try to see life through your child's eyes. Strive to give meaning to the environment and the everyday activities he encounters, from his perspective. The most effective strategies are those that you *individualize* for your child.

⚷ Provide meaning

Use strategies that are visual and easy to understand. Provide a sense of order, familiarity, and clarity. Take your cue from your child's strengths and interests. Make things meaningful from *his* point of view.

When an event or a situation has meaning, all sorts of undesirable behaviors frequently drop away. Most important, learning is free to take place when the world—his activities and the environment—make sense. Most people, young and old, with autism or not, are happier when things make sense; we are at peace when our lives have meaning.

⚷ Individualize

Usually, when visually structured strategies are tried, there is almost always an immediate positive impact. However, the most exciting *ongoing results* occur when the basic strategies are fine-tuned to fit the individual.

Obviously, the author does not know your child. Though you might find an idea in this book which will work exactly as described, it is more likely that you will need to make it fit your child and his particular situation. Try it, observe what happens, adapt accordingly, try it again, see how it works, adapt again, try it again, and on and on. The "right" strategies and the "right" adaptations become apparent as you proceed. *Your child will show you what works and what needs changing through his successes and his frustrations.*

Every child (and family or classroom) is unique. The process of assessment, structuring, reassessment, and adaptation, referred to by TEACCH as *restructuring*, allows for the merging of your experience, intuition and knowledge of your child, with objective observation.

There is no single recipe that works for everyone. Real effectiveness of the structured teaching strategies presented here depends on our ability to individualize for *this one child*.

Acknowledgements

I am grateful for the immense support I have received.

I first want to thank my colleagues and friends; the staff of the Asheville TEACCH Center for their support during the writing of this book. This multi-talented group of people cheerfully took over my responsibilities when I took time off. Thank you to: Anne McGuire, my office-mate, who faithfully protected me by never letting me *really* know just how busy it got; Sloane Burgess, who listened carefully, giving me her opinions whenever I asked even if she was in the middle of her own writing; Galene Fraley, my first mentor when I was new to autism, and whom I continue to learn from every time we work together; Ron Larsen, who helps me see things from a fresh perspective right at the moment I need one; Sara Handlan, whose quick thinking rescued me during a computer crisis; and Katie Craver, who introduced the workbook at Dickson School. Thank you to our office staff: Pat Greene, who finally admitted that she *really did* miss me when I was gone; Suzie Heaton, who took the time out of her busy life to read an early version of the book and made helpful suggestions from a parent's point of view; and Judy Hunter, who always checked on my progress.

And a big thank you to the Director of the Asheville TEACCH Center, Steve Love, Ph.D., who with his never-faltering positive attitude, has supported every project I have come to him with, even if *this* one meant taking time off.

Thank you to the TEACCH Program at large for being some of the nicest, most creative, and down-to-earth people there are. Thank you to Eric Schopler, Ph.D., founder and first TEACCH Director, for his humanity and genius. Thank you to Gary Mesibov, Ph.D., Director of TEACCH, for helping us understand autism as a culture, and for his insight, advice, and patient replies to my e-mails. And thank you to Roger Cox, Ph.D., our former director in Asheville, for his passionate presentations about social relatedness in autism.

Thank you to Cristina Webb for field testing this book at Isaac Dickson School in Asheville, NC, with her nine- to thirteen-year old students; and for sending me samples of her structured tasks when I was pondering what to include. Thank you to Jack Wall, Ph.D., Director of the Charlotte TEACCH Center, for permission to include *Mind the Gap*, and to Teresa Johnson for her help in describing the details of its use. And to my friend, Linda Larsen, for so quickly drawing a diagram of the "office".

Thank you to Vaya Papageorgiou, M.D., Ph.D. in Thessaloniki, Greece, for knowing I was going to write this book even before *I* knew it; and for translating it into Greek. And thank you to Cathy Pratt, Ph.D., in Indiana, and to Carol Gray in Michigan, for permission to include their inspiring work.

Thank you to the talented young artists who contributed drawings from their extensive collections: Paul Hoyt, Brian Davis, and Doug Buckner; and to their mothers: Gale Hoyt, Laurie Davis, and Gladys Buckner.

A very special thank you to the two artists who took on assignments. Their labor and creativity gave life to the pages of this book. Thomas Johnson, with thoughtfulness, dedication, and a pencil that comes alive with a positive attitude, drew seventy sketches just for this book. And to his mother, Teresa, who searched through boxes of his early drawings. To Maria White, who with deep personal committment, created six beautiful illustrations. I appreciate Maria's straightforward spirit and permission to quote her throughout the text.

Thank you to Dave Spicer for his commitment to educate about what it feels like to have autism and for writing his thoughts about artistic talent; to John Engle for editing the workbook pages and sharing his experiences so candidly; to Kelly Davis for her enthusiasm and clarity in editing the sections for parents and teachers; to our photographer, Marilyn Ferikes, who captured the unique spirits of the contributors in the photos at the back of the book; and to Adela Allen from the University of Arizona for permission to begin the book with her quote.

Thank you to the many children, families, and adults with autism whom I have the privilege of knowing. You have truly enriched my life. I humbly thank you for giving me an intimate view of the fascinating culture of autism.

Thank you to my cousin, Irene Vassos, for welcoming innumerable marathon weeks in front of the computer, formatting, scanning, inserting, evaluating, and reevaluating the visual presentation. It is Irene's eyes and skills behind this book's visual appeal. And thank you to Wayne Gilpin and *Future Horizons* who worked with me to get this book into your hands.

Thank you to Kemper Brown and Ken Jones of the *Electronic Office*, who patiently picked me up from the depths of despair during a computer crisis, and whose expertise made it possible to continue. To family and friends, who believed in this project and cheered me on; especially Odette, David, Michele, Joe, Jan, Dayna, Jim, Janna, Stuart, Helena, Bob, Tom, Maria, Mickey, Pandora, Bill, Claudia, Boone, Mom and Dad Faherty, and of course, Ed and Sheila.

And finally, thank you to the following members of my family for their unconditional support, without which this project would not have happened. To my mother who gave me creativity, stamina, and drive; to my father who taught me empathy and the importance of service; to both of them for the belief they instilled in me: *"for every problem there is a solution"*; to Aunt Jane who is visualizing this book as required reading for education majors; to my husband who teaches me everyday about selflessness; and to my son who reminds me about trust and faith in oneself; I am forever grateful.

Chapter 1: Introduction

Workbook

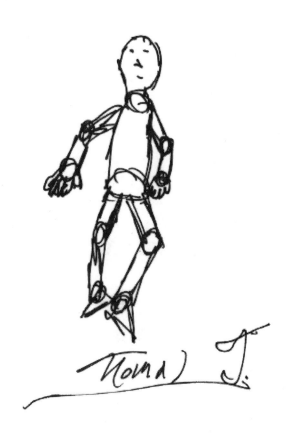

Thomas Johnson, 1999
Age 10

Introduction

I Might Have Questions

This book can help me understand myself better. I have been told that I have **high functioning autism** or **PDD** or **Asperger Syndrome** or **PDD-NOS** or _____.
I might have questions.

I will (circle) the questions that I have:

What does it mean?

Is there something wrong with me?

Am I the only one like this?

Isn't everyone like me?

Are there other people like me?

Who should I tell about this?

I might not have any questions. That is OK. But, if I have more questions, I can write them on the next page, or I can have someone write them for me.

If I have more questions, I can write them here.

I might not have questions now, but if I have some later, I can turn to this page and write them here.

1. _____ ?

2. _____ ?

3. _____ ?

4. _____ ?

5. _____ ?

6. _____ ?

7. _____ ?

8. _____ ?

9. _____ ?

10. _____ ?

11. _____ ?

12. _____ ?

Reading This Book

I can read this book with my parent or another adult who knows me well. I will read this book with:

♦ my parent

♦ my teacher

♦ someone else: _____

📖 Later, I can read it by myself. There might be certain pages that I like to read. Sometimes my parent or teacher might want to read particular pages with me, again.

Other people might like to read this book, too. I might share this book with one or all of these people:

♦ my grandparents

♦ my aunts and uncles

♦ my brother or sister

♦ my cousins

♦ my teacher

♦ my friend

♦ someone else: _____

This Is A Workbook

This is a workbook. It is OK to write on the pages. There are places to mark, blank lines to write on, and things to circle.

Every page has a number at the bottom. After reading a page, I can think about what I read. If there is something I want to remember, or if the page is important to me, I can draw a circle around the page number on the dotted line, like this ———

When I have finished reading this book, the page numbers that are circled will mark what is important to me.

These pages will help other people understand me better.

The Directions

Some pages in this book have things to read and mark. There might be blank lines to write on, or sentences to mark with a pen or pencil.

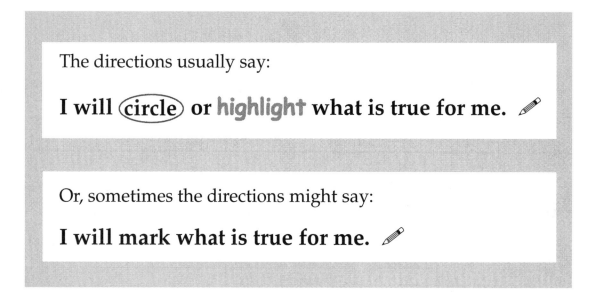

The directions usually say:

I will (circle) or highlight what is true for me.

Or, sometimes the directions might say:

I will mark what is true for me.

In this book, **mark** means to highlight or (circle).

We can **mark** the pages of this book with a colored highlighter pen...

highlighting through the words like this.

or, we can **mark** with a regular pen or pencil, like this...

circling or drawing a line around the words

Practice Marking What Is True

Different things are true for different children. Every child who has a workbook like this might mark different things.

On this page, I can practice filling in the blank lines and marking what is true. I will only mark or write things that are true for me. If the statement is not true for me, I will not mark it.

I will ⟨circle⟩ or highlight what is true for me. ✎

- ▶ I am a boy.
- ▶ I am a girl.
- ▶ I am one million years old.
- ▶ I am ten years old.
- ▶ I am _____ years old.
- ▶ I live in North Carolina.
- ▶ I live in the USA. I live in the state of _____.
- ▶ I do not live in the USA. I live in _____.
- ▶ I like to eat pizza.
- ▶ I do not like to swim.
- ▶ I like to swim.
- ▶ I do not have a sister.
- ▶ I have a sister.

My _____ is reading this page with me.

On Saturday, I want to _____.

Special Practice Sheet

My parent or teacher can prepare this special practice sheet by writing sentences on the blank lines. Some are true for me, and some are not true for me.

I will (circle) or highlight what is true for me. 🖉

- ▶ I like to read.
- ▶ I do not like to read.
- ▶ I have a sister.
- ▶ I have a brother.
- ▶ I am the oldest child in my family.
- ▶ I am the youngest child in my family.

- ▶ _____
- ▶ _____
- ▶ _____
- ▶ _____
- ▶ _____
- ▶ _____
- ▶ _____
- ▶ _____
- ▶ _____
- ▶ _____
- ▶ _____
- ▶ _____

Introducing Me

My name is _____.

My birthday is _____.

Today's date is _____.

I will draw a picture (or tape a photo) of myself, here.

Strengths and Talents

Everyone has strengths and talents. My strengths and talents are things that I can do well and enjoy doing.

I will (circle) or highlight what is true for me. ✏

My strengths or talents are:

- reading
- spelling
- alphabetical order
- handwriting or calligraphy
- foreign languages
- drawing or painting
- computers
- addition or subtraction
- multiplication or division
- matching
- dates
- numerical orders
- playing a musical instrument
- facts about: _____
- singing on perfect pitch
- memory
- remembering how things look

- writing stories or poetry
- photography
- sports
- cooking or baking
- cleaning
- straightening up
- putting things in order
- drama
- mechanical things
- constructing things
- understanding animals
- sewing, knitting, or weaving
- algebra
- other:_____
- other:_____

Autism Is Another Thing About Me

Another thing about me is that **I have autism**. Most children do not have autism, but some do. I am one of the children who has autism.

There are children and adults all over the world who have autism. I might not know any other people who have autism, but maybe someday I will meet others.

People with autism are different from each other. Some children with autism never talk. Some talk a little and some talk a lot!

I have a special kind of autism called **high functioning autism** or **Asperger Syndrome**. Sometimes it is called **PDD** or **PDDNOS**. It can be called an **Autism Spectrum Disorder**. All of these terms are related to autism.

In this book, it is just called **autism**, but it can mean all these things:

▶ High Functioning Autism

▶ Asperger Syndrome *(or Aspergers)*

▶ PDD *(Pervasive Developmental Disorder)*

▶ PDDNOS *(Pervasive Developmental Disorder Not Otherwise Specified)*

▶ Autism Spectrum Disorder *(or ASD)*

▶ other: _____

On the list above, my parent will circle **or** highlight **the terms that have been used with me.** 🖉

What Is Autism?

Autism is invisible. No one can see autism. It is one of the things that make me who I am. This book will explain what is special about autism.

Autism affects the way my brain works. The brain is like a computer which is always on and keeps people living and learning. Autism causes my brain to sometimes work differently than other people's brains.

Having a brain with autism is like having a computer with an *Autism Operating System (AOS)*, while most other people have a *Plain Operating System (POS)**.

Autism makes me experience the world in a certain way. Sometimes it's the same as most people, but sometimes I experience the world differently.

Autism is another way of thinking and being.

---

*Autism Operating System analogy by Ellen Tanis, parent of a boy with Asperger Syndrome. She suggested to her son that perhaps he had an ASOS (Asperger Syndrome Operating System) while other people have a POS (Plain Operating System). Ms. Tanis' delightful essay was published on page 15 of the Fall 1996 issue of *The Morning News*, an excellent resource and quarterly publication by Carol Gray. Subscription information can be found in the *Recommended Resources* at the end of the book.

Introduction

Why Do I Have Autism?

No one knows why I have autism. Scientists are not sure what causes autism in particular people. They are trying to find out why some children have autism and others do not. Autism is still a mystery. But they do know *some* things about it.

Scientists know that:

- Autism is not a disease, and it does not mean that I am sick.

- It does not mean that I am bad or wrong, *or* that I am better than other children.

- It is nobody's fault that I have autism.

- Autism is called *neurological* because it involves my brain.

- Sometimes it appears to be genetic. Cousins, uncles, aunts, brothers, sisters, or other family members might also have autism.

**It is not wrong or bad to have autism.
Autism is another way of thinking and being.**

Introduction

Was I Born With Autism?

My parent and I can fill in the spaces below. 🖉

When I was born, my parent(s) and the doctor did not know that I had autism. No one can tell if a baby has autism. They did not expect me to have autism, because most babies do not have autism.

My parent(s) first thought that there was something a little different about me when I was ___ years old, but they still did not know that I had autism. They loved me very much and they did not understand why I ...

_____

_____

_____

_____ .

My parent(s) found out that I had autism when I was _____ years old. Then they understood more about me. They kept on loving me very much.

Now, *I* know that I have autism. I am _____ years old. My parent(s) gave me this book to help me understand myself better. They want me to know that I am a special and wonderful person. ❤

For Parents and Teachers

An introductory message from an adult with autism:

As an autistic person who went undiagnosed until age 46 (in 1994), I have watched with gratitude as the body of knowledge concerning autism has grown in recent years. Not only are there many more books describing autism from an academic, medical, or parental perspective, but also an increasing number of autistic people are adding their own views, experiences, and insights to the available literature.

This book offers another approach to furthering the understanding of autism: that of encouraging autistic children to learn more about themselves and guiding them through a journey of self-discovery. The workbook is a valuable resource for autistic children's awareness and understanding of their natures, as well as for their self-esteem. Such a book could have been very helpful to me and to my family when I was a child.

With best wishes,

Dave Spicer
April 1999
Asheville, North Carolina

The introductory workbook chapter acknowledged that the reader has heard "autism" or a related diagnostic term applied to him, and offered simple explanations. It set the tone for the workbook, and helped the adult helper assess the child's ability to accurately describe himself by marking what is true and by filling in personal information where indicated.

Ideas in This Chapter

✓ Marking what is true

✓ The workbook requires your partnership and guidance

✓ What if your child wants to mark all the options, or won't mark any of them?

✓ Underline with a strip of paper to help focus

✓ Pick and choose which pages to read

Marking what is true

Many children with high functioning autism may not be able to identify, from a list of qualities, opinions, or descriptions, the things that apply to themselves. On the other hand, there are children and adolescents with autism or a related diagnosis who, with some teaching, practice, and encouragement, will be able to participate in marking and filling in accurate and insightful information.

Keep a pen, pencil, or light-colored highlighter pen available to use when marking the workbook pages.

The workbook requires your partnership and guidance

This workbook is meant to be completed with adult guidance. Because of the wide range of abilities and skills found among children with autism, the level and amount of support and direction that is needed from the adult will vary from child to child. In addition, much of the information presented on the workbook pages are meant for adult readers, as well.

What if your child wants to mark *all* the options, or won't mark *any* of them?

To help determine whether your child can accurately mark what is true, the first workbook chapter contains concrete instructions and practice pages. Use these pages as a teaching tool. You can refer back to them as needed, during the reading of the book. Some children may still routinely and indiscriminately continue to mark all the options as they progress through the book. Or, they may revert to marking all the options when they come across information that they do not comprehend. Some children insist upon marking what they perceive as the correct answers, whether or not they are really true. If your child has difficulty marking what is really true for him, you can try one or more of these suggestions:

☑ **You can highlight ahead of time.**

Before reading the book with your child, go through the lists with a highlighter pen and highlight the items which you know to be absolutely true about him. Then, as you read the book together, he can circle what is highlighted. *If you do this, be very careful to only highlight what you are absolutely sure of.* Even if you are leaving some options blank that may be true (but you aren't positive), it is better to leave them blank than to "put words in his mouth" that may not really be true.

☑ **Let him leave all the choices blank.**

Even if this book is read without marking anything, there is still enough critical information on any one page for a reader to benefit. Perhaps, as your child matures, he may develop his ability to self-reflect. Then later on, when he is ready, you can help him mark what is true.

☑ **Let him mark *all* the options, if he insists.**

The important thing is that he is interested in the book. You can read the book together again, later. Before the second reading, you can mark what you know to be true about your child. If he has circled, you can mark with a highlighter. If he has highlighted, you can circle. During the second reading he will notice what you have marked. *Keep in mind that you should only mark what you are absolutely sure of.*

☑ **Use the blank line, next to *"other:_____"***

At the bottom of most of the lists, a line labeled as *"other"*, has been left blank. Use this line in a way that is most helpful for your child. You can fill in what you know to be true, *or* it can be left blank. Your child might suggest what you should write, or he might write it himself. Then, it can be circled or highlighted, in the same way as the others. *If there is no blank line, but there is something that is true for your child which was not listed, you can simply draw a blank line, write what is true, and then circle or highlight.*

☑ **Talk about the lists, "...what is true for me."**

Start a dialogue and help your child understand if and how the relevant information on the lists might apply to him. Depending on your child's tolerance for talking with you about the issues, and his own ability to self-reflect, you may want to use some of the items on the lists to initiate a discussion. Of course for you, talking about the items may come naturally. It may not be so natural or easy for your child. If the discussion is upsetting to him, or if he resists at all, it would probably be better to let the book speak for itself. *Do not push for a "meaningful discussion" if it is upsetting or confusing to your child, no matter how important it might be from your point of view.* In some cases, it might be best if you let him explore the book in his own way, on his own terms. You also might try one of the previous suggestions above. Later on, you can try a written conversation about a specific topic, as suggested in Chapters 6 and 8.

Underline with a strip of paper to help him focus

There is a lot of visual information on the workbook pages. Most of the lists contain a number of options to read, think about, choose from, and mark. If I had insisted on making the workbook as visually clear as possible for all children, then I would have had to modify the pages in ways that might have stretched this book to at least ten times longer than it is! Not having done that, I suggest instead that you try this method—*cut a wide strip of paper and keep it with the book.*

When reading, *use the strip of paper to underline* what your child is reading, so it covers the rest of the text, as demonstrated here.

For some children, it helps if *previous* lines are covered up, also. If your child is distracted by the lines of text he has *already* read, then you can get a larger piece of paper and cut a "window" in it. The window should be as long as a line of text, and as thick as a few lines.

As demonstrated here, the window highlights what is currently being read. When it is time to read the next group of lines, move the window down.

Pick and choose

Some pages may not describe your child. Other pages will probably contain concepts beyond your child's current level of comprehension. There may be pages which might give an accurate description of a particular aspect of your child's unique personality or behavior, even though *he* might not be able to understand what is written. In these cases, you should allow or encourage your child to skip the page, while you make a mental note to yourself to "earmark" it for his teachers' or other family members' enlightenment.

Chapter 2: Ways of Thinking

Workbook

Drawing by Maria White, 1999
Age 21

Special Interests

Everyone has interests, things they like. **One of the important things about having autism is that it helps me be very focused on my interests.** I usually feel good when I am focused on my special interests. I might have just one special interest or I might have more than one.

My favorite special interests are:

1. _____

2. _____

3. _____

There are many ways to enjoy special interests. **I will mark the ways I like to enjoy my special interests.** 🖉

> ▶ I like to **think** about my special interests.
> ▶ I like to **read** about my special interests.
> ▶ I like to **talk** about my special interests.
> ▶ I like to **draw** pictures about my special interests.
> ▶ I like to **write** about my special interests.
> ▶ I like to **do something** with my special interests.

Some children with autism have the same special interests for a long time. Sometimes special interests change after a few months. On the next page is a list of my special interests over the last few years.

These are my special interests over the past few years:

1. _____

2. _____

3. _____

4. _____

5. _____

6. _____

7. _____

8. _____

(Add more numbers if needed.)

_____

_____

_____

_____

_____

_____

Details

Sometimes people say that I have a *good memory*.

Many children with autism have good memories. The kinds of things that children with autism notice and remember are called **details**. *Details can be colors, letters, numbers, shapes, places, names, signs, smells, sounds, dates, times, phone numbers, and many other things.* Some of the details I notice are things that other people don't think are important, so they might not notice or remember them.

I usually remember details that are interesting to me, or that are related to my special interests. Some details that I notice and remember are:

1. _____

2. _____

3. _____

4. _____

**Most children with autism
are good at noticing and remembering details
that are important to them.**

Ways of Thinking

Styles of Learning

Everyone learns. Sometimes learning is easy and sometimes learning is difficult. Children learn in different ways. Everyone has his or her own **style of learning**. Autism affects my style of learning.

I will ⟨circle⟩ or highlight what is true for me.

I like it when:

▶ I can watch what people are doing.

▶ There are pictures I can see.

▶ There are words I can read.

▶ Someone reads to me.

▶ It's my special interest.

▶ People talk a lot.

▶ other: _____

I learn more easily when I read the words,

rather than when I listen to someone talk.

↑

If this is true for me, then I will ⟨circle⟩ this statement. If it is not true, then I will ~~cross it out~~.

Ways of Thinking

Perfection

Many children with autism like things to be **perfect**. This is why many children with autism are good workers, but sometimes it can cause problems.

I will ⬭circle⬭ or highlight what is true for me. ✏

▶ I want to be the first one finished with my work.

▶ I want my work to look a certain way, so I keep correcting it over and over again.

▶ I erase my work many times.

▶ I do not want to see any mistakes on my work.

▶ If it doesn't look right, I give up and get anxious or angry.

▶ Other: _____

But everything cannot always be perfect. I am not wrong or bad if other children are first, or if I make mistakes. *Everyone* makes mistakes, even the smartest people in the world. I can try to:

• let it be OK if **someone else** finishes first. I can finish second or third or later.

• correct the mistakes that I know how to correct.

• **ask** someone for help with the mistakes I don't understand.

• **continue** with the activity or assignment.

• other: _____

I do not need to start over from the beginning, again and again. I do not need to feel bad about my work.

Ways of Thinking

*More on **perfection**...*

If having to be first, or having to start my work over and over again, cause problems for me, I can try keeping a list. If it helps, then my parent or teacher can make more lists for me to use.

I will record the date every time that I let someone else be first.

1. I let someone else be first on _____ .

2. I let someone else be first on _____ .

3. I let someone else be first on _____ .

4. I let someone else be first on _____ .

I will record the date every time I finish my work, instead of erasing and starting over and over.

1. I didn't start over, again. I was finished, on _____ .

2. I didn't start over, again. I was finished, on _____ .

3. I didn't start over, again. I was finished, on _____ .

4. I didn't start over, again. I was finished, on _____ .

My parent or teacher can fill in the blanks with something that I can practice.

I will record the date every time I _____ .

1. _____ .

2. _____ .

3. _____ .

Ways of Thinking

Routines and Familiarity

Children with autism like routines and familiarity. A **routine** is when I do the same things in the same ways. **Familiarity** means being used to something.

Routines make me feel good because I know what to expect. I like to know what is going to happen and when it will happen. I usually feel better when things are familiar to me.

I like these things to *stay the same:*

1. _____

2. _____

3. _____

4. _____

5. _____

6. _____

Sometimes things have to change. Unexpected things happen in life. Sometimes I know ahead of time that things will be different.

Sometimes I don't know that there is going to be a change until it happens.

Changes

Sometimes I am focused on my special interest and I don't want to stop. Or something may be familiar and I don't want it to **change.**

But someone might say that it is time to do something else, or that **things have changed.** Sometimes there is a **surprise.**

Many children like surprises. Surprises are when things change unexpectedly, and *we do not know exactly how they will change.* Many children think that surprises are fun, but most children with autism think it is more fun for things to stay the same.

When things change or are new or different, I might wonder if they will ever be the same again.

When things change, I might feel anxious, confused, sad, frustrated or angry. **Changes might be difficult for children with autism.**

I can write down some of the changes that bother me on the next page.

I do not have to write on all the lines. I just have to write what is true for me.

Some changes that bother me are:

1. _____ .

2. _____ .

3. _____ .

4. _____ .

5. _____ .

6. _____ .

7. _____ .

8. _____ .

9. _____ .

10. _____ .

11. _____ .

12. _____ .

A Schedule Can Help Me Be Flexible

Everything cannot always stay the same. **Being flexible** means that when things change, I will not get too upset. Children who are flexible can have fun even when things change. Following a **schedule** can help me be flexible.

A **schedule** is a list of what is going to happen today. Using a schedule is fun. When I look at the schedule,

- I *know* which things will be the *same* as usual today, and which things are going to be *different*.

- I can *see* if a *surprise* is going to happen.

- I can *see* what is going to happen *first* and what is going to happen *later*.

- I know that *I will not be stuck doing something I don't like* because I can see that it will end and that something else will happen next.

- I can see when it is going to be time for my *special interests*.

- I am *involved*. When I check my schedule, I find out what is going to happen next. I mark each thing as I do it.

Last-Minute Changes

Sometimes things have to change unexpectedly. It might change right away, or it might change soon. An unexpected change is also called a **last-minute change.**

If there are *last-minute changes*, my parent or teacher can go to my schedule, and erase or cross out what was supposed to happen. Then they can write the change on my schedule.

Even if something is going to change soon, it can still be written on my schedule, so I can see when something is going to be different. *It is easier for me to understand and handle changes when I can see what is going to happen.*

If I do not have a schedule, then my parent or teacher can help me cope with a last minute change by writing a note and giving it to me.

The last minute-change might be easier to deal with, if I read about it. *Then I can keep the note with me, and check again, whenever I want.*

Examples of schedules used in a variety of situations, are at the end of this chapter in the section: *For Parents and Teachers*, pages 44-49.

For Parents and Teachers

"I would have liked it if I could have made better sense out of what was happening...if there was some kind of order or predictability that I could have relied on."

-Dave Spicer at 49, talking about his childhood

Ideas in This Chapter

✓ The need for success

✓ Assessment

✓ Daily informal assessment

✓ Inconsistency

✓ Visually structured teaching

✓ The schedule

1. Why use a schedule?
2. Individualizing the schedule
3. How do I make a schedule?
4. How long a period of time should it cover?
5. Do I need to write the *times* on the schedule?
6. Keep it clear and easy to read
7. How can the schedule teach him to be more flexible?
8. How can it help him stay organized?
9. Check-boxes, check-lines, or crossing through
10. How can the schedule help us deal with his restricted interests?
11. How can the schedule help us neutralize arguments?
12. What if he is not interested in using the schedule?
13. Incorporating the schedule as part of life
14. Is the goal for him to write his own schedule?
15. To use or not to use?

The need for success

Most of us learn through trial and error. Life presents us with opportunity to learn through our mistakes as well as through our successes. We remember what to do differently *next time.* We understand the connection between our behavior and its consequences. This process works so naturally that many current parenting manuals suggest discipline methods which promote situations that allow children to learn through the consequences of their actions.

In contrast, learning by trial and error can be so unpredictable and even frightening to children with autism that they become *unwilling to try.* Many parents of children with autism have watched as their child avoids involvement in an activity until he or she can do it perfectly.

It has been observed that the need for success among many children with autism is immediate and total. They are so averse to making mistakes that many don't risk trying until they are sure that they can do it perfectly and flawlessly, without failing. **They don't easily learn from mistakes, nor do they see the connections, the process, and the relationship between making a mistake, almost succeeding, and achievement.**

To expect a child with high functioning autism to learn only through the natural events of trial and error is to risk raising a child whose self-image is sacrificed to a feeling of shame and harsh self-judgment. Children who see only polarities (good/bad, black/white, right/wrong) naturally will come to the conclusion that they are bad or wrong when they make a mistake. One adult with autism said that as a child, he perceived life as "failure after failure."

Mistakes are an unavoidable part of life for all of us. However autism, with its distinctive characteristics, automatically causes a higher degree of ill-timed behavior, awkwardness, and sometimes, total misunderstanding. Consequently, children with autism experience even *more* mistakes than the average child! The fact that they do not make connections between their behavior and its consequences, and that they do not easily learn from their mistakes, only 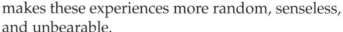 makes these experiences more random, senseless, and unbearable.

The teaching strategies that parents and teachers of children with autism rely on must embrace the principle of building on a solid foundation of mastered skills and competence. Daily observation and constant assessment are essential. Teaching strategies that are designed to prevent failure and reinforce accomplishment will help to ensure that learning is free to take place.

Assessment

An overall assessment of your child's skills and pattern of learning is necessary. Formal and informal assessment will reveal his unique pattern of strengths and weaknesses, talents, and interests. No single numerical score (and no single test) can accurately describe your child's development. Children with autism have "peaks and valleys" in their development. Nonverbal skills may be more developed than verbal skills, although among many high functioning children and those with Asperger Syndrome, verbal skills are often highly developed while deficits will be seen in some of the nonverbal skill areas. Even within these two general areas, development will be scattered. Adaptive functioning scores (how the child does in the real, everyday world) are typically much lower than cognitive (thinking) skills.

Your child's particular pattern of development, strengths and needs, style of learning, and special interests must be taken into account when planning his educational program.

Daily informal assessment

Your careful observations from day to day, and activity to activity, constitute some of the most valuable assessment information about your child. What triggers anxiety? anger? withdrawal? What captures his interest? When is he the calmest? What strategies help him be most organized? cooperative? involved?

Your detailed observations can be used when developing teaching strategies and individualizing his educational program.

Inconsistency

Many parents have said that the only thing consistent about their child is the fact that he is *inconsistent!* "Peaks and valleys" of development and difficulty generalizing what is learned in one situation to another situation, are hallmark characteristics of autism. Being able to do one thing, on one day, does not ensure that he will be able to repeat it the next time. It is tempting to explain such inconsistent behavior with statements like *"he is just being manipulative"* or *"he can do it if he wants to."*

It is important to remember that in most cases, when a child with autism cannot or is not doing something, it usually means that there is something about the activity that is confusing or doesn't make sense to him–*even if he was successful at it yesterday.* Small changes in the external environment such as a different teacher, different location, different materials, or too much stimulation, can make a major difference. Variations in his internal state, such as feeling tired, sick, anxious, or distracted by other thoughts, can cause a dramatic change in how he performs.

Remember that inconsistency is a part of his style of learning. Accepting his puzzling behavior at face value, instead of jumping to conclusions about his motives, will help teachers and parents look at his behaviors in a fresh light. Observe what is. Using teaching methods which offer consistency in his external environment can be a place to start.

Visually structured teaching

In order to maximize his learning potential, any methods for teaching new skills and managing behavior must be tailored to the way your child learns. Most children with high functioning autism respond positively to visually structured teaching methods. Even when a child's verbal skills are more developed than his nonverbal skills, structured teaching techniques can be reassuring and help him organize, focus, sequence, and therefore function more independently. For those children who may have weak visual processing skills, such as children with nonverbal learning disabilities, structured teaching adds at least an organizational element and can promote independent skills. One of the most effective visually structured teaching strategies is the *individualized daily schedule.*

The schedule

An effective visual strategy that provides predictability while it teaches flexibility is an *individualized daily schedule.* The individualized schedule for students with autism has been developed and widely used by the TEACCH Program since the 1970s. Visual schedules help children and adults with autism anticipate and prepare for activities throughout the day. Transitions and changes become easier, expectations are clearer, and the child becomes more organized. Schedules can be used for school, home, and outings.

Typically, children and adults with high functioning autism respond best to a schedule that has been written or typed. Sometimes, the inclusion of symbols or pictures, paired with the written information, can clarify and reassure.

It is important to note that when we refer to "the schedule," we are not referring to the actual activities themselves, nor to a prescribed sequence of daily activities. "The schedule" refers simply to the visual strategy which clarifies what activities will occur, and in what order they will occur. Examples of schedules can be found on pages 44-49.

1. Why use a schedule?

When used consistently, the schedule is a valuable strategy which can result in many positive short- and long-term changes. Using an individual schedule:

✓ Capitalizes on visual strengths

✓ Promotes independence

✓ Rations time for special interests

✓ Teaches flexibility

✓ Builds necessary vocational skills

✓ Helps an argumentative child more easily accept directions from others

2. Individualizing the schedule

As with all teaching methods, success lies with the adult's ability to individualize for each child. Perhaps even more essential to the teaching of children with autism than with typically developing children, gearing the strategy to the individual often determines their success or failure.

The rest of this chapter suggests the various issues to be considered when individualizing a schedule for your child.

3. How do I make a schedule?

A written schedule is comparable to an adult's calendar or appointment book. It must be easily accessible. Use a note pad, stenographers' notebook, spiral notebook or clipboard. Some children clip the current day's school schedule onto the front of their loose-leaf binder.

Write your child's schedule at the beginning of the day, listing the activities and events in sequence. Include favorite activities as well as the things he resists doing. Be specific enough so he can see any change from the usual routine. Add relevant details to avoid confusion.

4. How long of a period of time should it cover?

After using the schedule for a while with your child, carefully observe the optimum number of items on the list that he can handle at one time. For some children, seeing all of the day's events at the same time is too distracting. If this is the case, write only the sequence of events for the morning. At noon start a fresh schedule by listing the afternoon's activities in sequence.

On the other hand, there are some children who may become distressed if they can't see the entire day's plan from the beginning to end. These children might function better when shown a full day's schedule all at once.

Some parents use a schedule at home just to get through the "rough spots"—for example, a certain time during the day that causes their child the most distress or frustration. This can help on weekends in particular, when the nature of the day may be unstructured, or when there's a possibility of last-minute changes in plans.

5. Do I need to write the *times* on the schedule?

Include the actual "clock time" if it is helpful and not distressing to your child when things don't happen exactly on time. Simply showing the sequence of

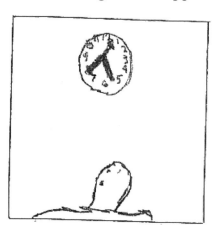

events, without the times, often works well enough. A single schedule frequently has a combination of entries; some defined by a specific time, and others which are not.

Many children have learned the meaning of "approximately" through the consistent use of the schedule with "approximate times." Using visual cues, such as color coding a 20-minute range of time on a picture of a clock, can help clarify the meaning of "approximate."

6. Keep it clear and easy to read

The visual information should be simple, clear, and concise. *Use words, symbols, or pictures which your child can understand as effortlessly as possible.* Use what he will recognize most easily on his "worst days," when he is the most anxious. One- or two-word entries, or short phrases, are often all that is needed.

Make sure that the list is visually clear, keeping it orderly and leaving enough space between the lines to clarify the separate entries.

Depending on your child's response to the schedule, you might need to highlight or underline key words, drawing his attention to the most important information.

7.   How can the schedule teach him to be more flexible?

When changes need to occur or additions need to be made after the schedule has already been given to the child, you can revise the schedule "on the spot." Explain the change clearly and simply in a matter-of-fact tone of voice, while you cross out and/or add the change on the schedule. Keep in mind that you want to simultaneously pair verbal information *(talking)* with visual information *(writing on the schedule)* so this new information can be processed easily.

As he becomes more familiar with using a schedule, he will more easily adapt to changes. After all, they are indicated on the schedule!

8.   How can it help him stay organized?

Make sure that your child has easy access to a pen or pencil so he can mark the schedule at each transition. Sometimes keeping the schedule on a clipboard, and hanging a pencil or pen on a clipboard with a string, or attaching it to a spot of Velcro, is most convenient. *Teach the child to check off or cross out each entry as the day progresses.* This clarifies the passage of time and keeps him organized. It also promotes independence by giving the child an active role in staying on track.

9.   Check-boxes, check-lines, or crossing through

Providing **check-boxes** on the schedule clarifies and defines the act of "checking the schedule." Seeing the empty check boxes will remind him that there are specific things to do, and that he will be checking them off as he moves through the day. A **short line** in the margin next to each entry is another way to structure "checking off." Other children can learn to **cross a line through** each entry as they begin or complete the activity.

Those of us who use "to-do" lists typically cross them out *after* each errand is completed. However, when teaching your child to mark his schedule, another option that might work better is to check off or cross out each activity *before* beginning. This way; after an activity is completed, he can look back on the schedule and instantly notice the next unmarked entry on the list. This unmarked entry clearly shows "what is next" on the schedule, and reminds him what to do to get started; *he needs to check the box, and then begin by doing what it says.*

10. How can the schedule help us deal with his restricted interests?

Some children want to talk about one subject or do one thing exclusively. The structure of the schedule can help them participate in other activities while it "rations" time with the favorite subject. They can see that they *can* engage in their special interest, and exactly *when* they can engage in their special interest, because it is on the schedule one or more times, as part of the day's plan.

When your child insists on talking about a favorite theme beyond what is an appropriate length of time or frequency, simply refer to the schedule and point out *when*, during the day, he can talk about his special interest.

Or, if time for the special interest or favorite theme has not been written on the schedule at all, or not frequently enough, you can add it in, on the spot, following the same procedure for making a last-minute change or addition to the schedule. *(See the heading "How can the schedule teach him to be more flexible?" p. 36.)*

11. How can the schedule help us neutralize arguments?

Some children and their parents or teachers have developed a verbal routine of *arguing* or unproductive *back-and-forth questions and explanations.* Despite your most well-intentioned desires to "not get sucked in," you may find yourself arguing or trying unsuccessfully to explain why something is or is not happening.

The schedule can help change even the most firmly established patterns of arguing in a way that is non-threatening to both child and adult. The schedule allows the adult to be directive without appearing confrontational from the child's point of view. The child's attention is drawn to the fact that **"the schedule says..."** rather than on the adult who is telling him what to do, or on a familiar pattern of words that the adult usually uses. The fact that you are presenting information in a visual—and not strictly verbal—manner creates a greater ease with which the child can receive, process, understand, and accept new information.

In trying to break a well-established argumentative routine, the adult can try quietly handing the schedule and pencil to the child, without making eye contact. Keep your focus on the schedule. In these cases, refrain from talking or responding verbally to your child's objections, but simply behave as if you assume the child will do what the schedule tells him to do. It may be that your explanations or threats (so predictable to your child) trigger his arguments and set the old routine in motion. Use a matter-of-fact, calm tone of voice. Look at the schedule, hand it to your child or place it near him, and say simply, **"the schedule says that...."**

For most children, stress will dramatically decrease if no one tries to talk or explain the issue. Try staying quiet, refer him to the schedule, and then perhaps walk away, giving him space.

Dealing with difficult behavior is covered in more detail, in Chapter 11.

12.   What if he is not interested in using the schedule?

Sometimes older children who have not yet developed the routine of using a schedule will resist it. Even a younger child might need extra motivation. Consider these ideas:

☺   Appeal to his special interest by drawing a border or adding an illustration (e.g., picture of a train, map of the USA, ...) that relates to his interest. You might try writing the schedule in a special "theme" notebook that relates to his special interest, or get a special pencil or pen to be used only for checking the schedule.

For example, if he is especially interested in flags of other countries, attach a miniature flag of his favorite country to the end of a pencil. The pencil is kept with the schedule and is used only for the purpose of checking the schedule.

☺   Some children are motivated by a bonus system. Each time he checks and follows his schedule, he earns a point. A certain number of points is good for a cash refund, video rental, or another activity that is particularly meaningful to your child.

☺   Have the school principal or other people in official roles, especially someone he particularily likes, show him their appointment book or day planner. Visit an office supply store and have him choose an "official" appointment book or day planner.

☺   There might be something about how the schedule looks which makes it visually unappealing or confusing to your child. Try simplifying it. Use one or two words for each entry. Leave enough space between the lines. Emphasize important information by highlighting or color coding.

13. Incorporating the schedule as part of life

The schedule can serve many purposes now and in the future. Use it daily, refer to it often, consult it when there are questions or issues, change it to reflect each day's uniqueness, and include it in everyday conversation to illustrate the things you are saying.

Refer to the schedule when there is discussion about what to do or when something will happen. Adapt your behavior or change the schedule accordingly. Help your child see it as a dynamic, valid, and trusted part of daily life. It will prove to be a valuable tool now and in the future.

In North Carolina, we have observed that the adults with autism who are most successful in keeping their jobs are those who are proficient in following a schedule and using other organizational strategies. The time to teach and practice these strategies is when the child is young and still in school.

14. Is the goal for him to write his own schedule?

Not necessarily. The goal is to teach him to *follow* a checklist to stay on track, be organized, and be able to function successfully in academic, social, and work situations. Even adults with autism function well when given checklists that are already written for them to follow, even if they cannot generate the list themselves due to inherent organizational difficulties. In fact, most are more successful at school or work when they follow the teacher's or supervisor's recommended sequence rather than their own idea of how a job should be done. Review the points on page 37.

15. To use or not to use?

Sometimes parents or teachers feel that a daily written schedule is not needed during the school day because their child "goes with the flow" or follows verbal directions easily. Or, after the schedule is used for a period of time, it is discarded because the child doesn't seem to need it anymore.

In these cases, it is tempting to decide that using a schedule, along with other visual strategies recommended later in this book, is not really appropriate for your child. On one hand, this may appear to be true. In school, he may respond to verbal directions and seem to cope with transitions. He may be able to wait, without too many questions, until there is time for him to engage in his special interests. Or, he may have memorized the routine of the school day and knows what is supposed to happen. He might be easy-going, seemingly unconcerned or unaware about upcoming events. He may get good grades, and achieve academically in some subjects *"better than other students."* After school though, it may be a different story.

> *One first grader with high functioning autism who was a "model student" would fall apart when he got home; wildly throwing whatever he could get his hands on.*

> *A quiet sixth grader with Asperger Syndrome, after getting picked up by his mother at the end of the school day, would get in the car and bang his head on the window.*

> *Upon arriving home after school, a fourth grader in a program for the gifted and talented would run upstairs to his room, strip off his clothes, and refuse to talk to anyone for the rest of the evening.*

> *A second grader, generally polite at school, would swear loudly and incessantly at home, calling his mother names.*

It is not uncommon for children with high functioning autism to perform well in school only to fall apart at home, as these examples illustrate. The amount of energy that it takes for children with autism to function successfully within the overstimulating and demanding school environment may be inconceivable to those of us with a neurological system unaffected by autism.

Structured teaching strategies, represented by the *schedule* in this chapter, offer predictability, familiarily, and clarity, resulting in an overall decreased level of anxiety. Along with the multiple uses already mentioned, "structure" is valued as a preventative behavior-management strategy because it helps children do the things they need to do all day, more easily, requiring less effort and stress.

Six Examples of Schedules

Schedule Example #1

Earlier this morning, Nick's teacher printed out today's schedule. The sequence and details vary from day to day. Certain words are bolded to get his attention. Nick checks each line, one at a time, before starting the activity. He keeps his schedule on a clipboard in his desk.

Note that his teacher had to make a last-minute change at 11:00.

Ms. Greene always follows the same procedure for *Science*, first presenting information to the entire class, followed by small group activities. When *Science* appears on Nick's schedule, she fills in the lines appropriately so he knows what to expect. Information about *school jobs* and *checklists* are on pp. 178, and 194-196.

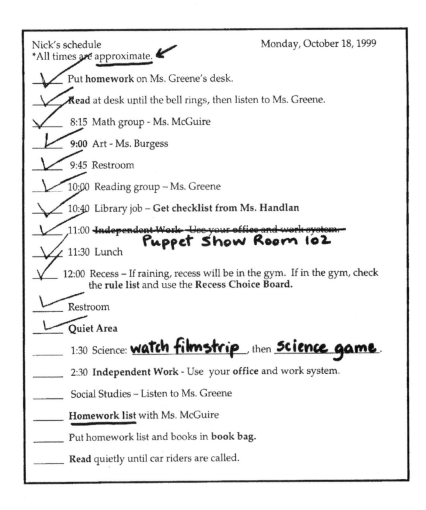

Nick's schedule   Monday, October 18, 1999
*All times are approximate.

___ Put **homework** on Ms. Greene's desk.

___ **Read** at desk until the bell rings, then listen to Ms. Greene.

___ 8:15 Math group - Ms. McGuire

___ 9:00 Art - Ms. Burgess

___ 9:45 Restroom

___ 10:00 Reading group – Ms. Greene

___ 10:40 Library job – **Get checklist from Ms. Handlan**

___ 11:00 ~~Independent Work - Use your office and work system.~~ **Puppet Show Room 102**

___ 11:30 Lunch

___ 12:00 Recess – If raining, recess will be in the gym. If in the gym, check the **rule list** and use the **Recess Choice Board.**

___ Restroom

___ **Quiet Area**

___ 1:30 Science: **watch filmstrip**, then **science game**.

___ 2:30 **Independent Work** - Use your **office** and work system.

___ Social Studies – Listen to Ms. Greene

___ **Homework list** with Ms. McGuire

___ Put homework list and books in **book bag.**

___ **Read** quietly until car riders are called.

Schedule Example #2

Ty's teacher writes his schedule by hand. Earlier in the day, she gave him his morning schedule, and now this one covers the afternoon. The sequence and details vary from day to day. Ty loves trains. He decorated the cover of a spiral notebook with train stickers in which his "train schedule" is written. He is motivated to use his schedule and mark it as the day progresses by coloring in the "train cars," an adaptation of check-boxes designed for him.

Note that his relaxation practice (which occurs right after lunch) is called "Train Trip." After the relaxation practice, Ty can make a choice of continuing to sit by himself in the *quiet area*, or join the other students at the busy after-lunch activities. This afternoon, Ty chose the Game Center instead of the *quiet area*.

Information about the *quiet area* can be found on pp. 64, 186, 211, 253, 260, 264; *relaxation* on pp. 256, 267; *mini-tramp* on pp. 255, 267; and *school job* on p. 178.

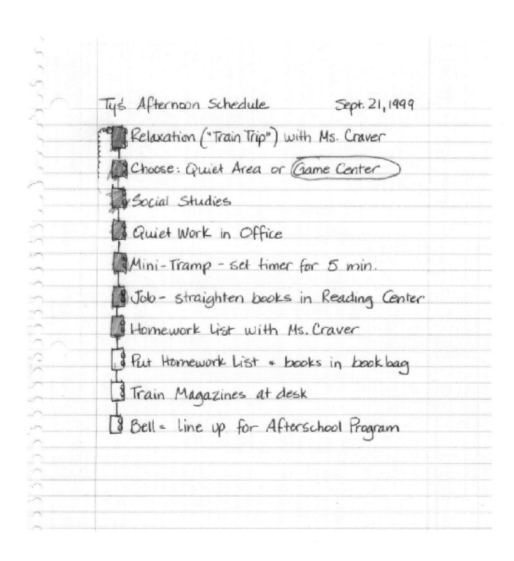

Schedule Example #3

Sometimes Catie can be very stressed after school. Her mother wrote this schedule by letting her begin the evening with solitary, less demanding activities: alone time, snack, and feeding the fish.

Catie loves fish. She is motivated by the *little fish* her mother draws on her schedule. There is a dot to the left of each line. This shows Catie where to put her pen to start drawing the line. She stops at the drawing of the little fish. In this way, Catie is motivated to accomplish and cross out each entry as she progresses through the evening.

Information can be found about *alone time* on p. 208; *homework* on p. 183; *checklists* on pp. 172-173; and *the calendar* on p. 96.

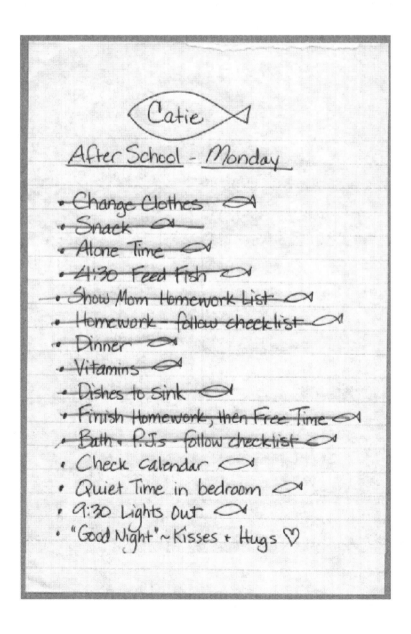

Schedule Example #4

Adam's mother wrote this schedule on both sides of an index card to help Adam prepare for an unusually busy and different day with the family.

Adam packed his swimming gear independently by checking the list under #3. He sees that there will be time for his favorite activities *(Nintendo or Legos)* after getting up and packing, and before leaving for Uncle Ron's house.

When the family arrived at Uncle Ron's house, they discovered that he wasn't planning to bring the raft because there was a large hole in it. Uncle Ron suggested that they build a sand castle, instead. Adam watched his mother as she wrote the change on his schedule.

He can see what will happen when the outing is finished–McDonald's, home, bath, and bed.

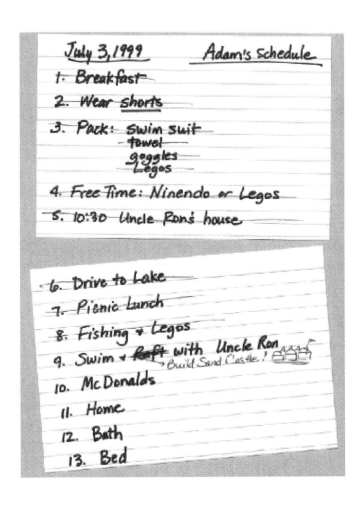

Schedule Example #5

Molly's summer day-camp counselor uses duplicates of the same form for the schedule every day, although the details change from day to day. Amy, the counselor, fills in the details of Molly's schedule before they meet at the beginning of the day. Molly is less anxious when she knows what to expect at camp.

Molly draws an "x" in each box as the day unfolds. Significant words for Molly have been bolded. Other words can be highlighted with a marker when needed. Note that at 1:00, the issue of rain has been addressed in a clear manner.

There are times when Molly is to make a choice. Choices have been indicated clearly on the schedule to clarify and ease her anxiety. Amy and Molly routinely circle her choices when they preview the schedule at the beginning of the day. Information about *free time* and *rules* can be found on pp. 179-182.

When I get to camp:

- ☒ Put lunch in the cooler.
- ☒ Meet with **Amy** to go over the schedule for today. 🚶
- ☒ **Quiet Area** – look over today's **schedule** by myself. 🗯

- ☒ 9:30 Group Meeting – listen to **Scott** 🗣
- ☒ 9:45 Morning exercises – Listen and watch 🚶 Carolyn
- ☒ 10:00 Outdoor activity: Obstacle Course
- ☒ 10:45 Snack. When finished, choose (Quiet Area) or Music Center
- ☒ 11:15 Arts and Crafts: ✂ paper mache masks
- ☒ 11:45 Bathroom. **Wash my hands.**
- ☒ 12:00 Lunch: 🍴 eat at red table
- ☒ 12:30 Free Time – Choose: (Uno) or Drawing
- ☒ 1:00 (**Not raining = POOL**) or **Raining = Indoor Games** Choose: balls or scooter boards
- ☒ 2:00 Bathroom
- ☐ 2:15 Snack. When finished, choose: **Quiet Area** or Game Center
- ☐ 2:45 **Get ready for home:** Get shell frame
- ☐ 3:00 Ride the yellow van home. 🚌

Schedule Example #6

Christopher's father wrote a schedule this afternoon to help Christopher handle the stress and uncertainty of leaving school early and going to the doctor. In addition, Christopher's father planned to stop in at a friend's house before going home.

Christopher can see that they are going to his favorite store after the appointment. Christopher knows what to expect to do in the waiting room, as well as what he can do at Ms. Fraley's house.

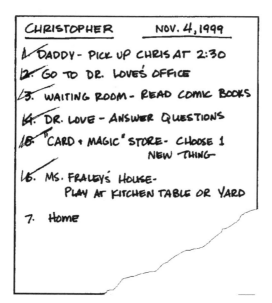

Chapter 3: The Sensory Experience
Workbook

Drawing by Thomas Johnson, 1992 and 1997
Ages 3 and 6

The Five Senses

There are five senses* . They are:

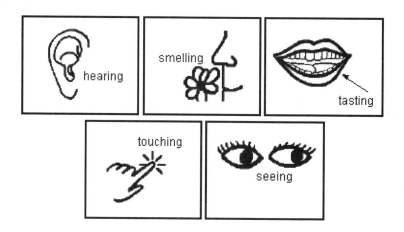

Everyone experiences the world through senses. Many children with autism experience their senses differently than children who do not have autism.

Sometimes what I experience through my senses feels good. Sometimes what I experience through my senses feels uncomfortable. Sometimes what I experience through my senses feels painful, or overwhelming. And sometimes I don't feel anything at all.

In this chapter, I will read, mark, and write what is true for me about my senses.

---

*Picture Communication Symbols © 1981-1999, Mayer-Johnson Company, are used with permission of the Mayer-Johnson Company.

Hearing Loud or Sudden Noises

Hearing is how everyone is aware of sounds in the world. Some loud or sudden noises that everyone hears are listed below. Most children aren't bothered by these noises, but many children with autism do not like some of them.

I will (circle) **or** highlight **the noises that bother me.** ✐

- ▶ vacuum cleaner
- ▶ telephone ringing
- ▶ school intercom
- ▶ lawn mower
- ▶ people talking at the same time
- ▶ babies crying
- ▶ car horns and sirens
- ▶ machines or motors starting up
- ▶ people coughing or laughing or yelling
- ▶ other: _____

There may be noises at home and at school and in other places that hurt my ears. *If this happens, I might become anxious.* Some children with autism might get angry or scared when they are anxious. They might yell or cry. They might feel like covering their ears and running away from the noise. **Sometimes loud or sudden noises make me want to** _____

_____ .

The Sensory Experience

Hearing Sounds Others Don't Notice

There are some sounds that I hear but other people do not seem to hear or they do not pay attention to them. Other people call them **quiet sounds,** but they are not always quiet to me. These are sounds like:

- birds and insects

- fluorescent lights, fans, refrigerators, computers

- airplanes or engines very far away

- radio or TV sounds in other rooms

- people talking or working in other rooms

- people breathing or turning pages near me

Most children do not pay attention to these kinds of sounds because the sounds are quiet to them. But children with autism often pay attention to these kinds of sounds. *Some of these sounds bother me.* Sometimes these sounds can hurt my ears or make me anxious.

Some of the **quiet sounds** that bother me are: _____

_____

_____ .

The Sensory Experience

Touching

Touching is what I feel when things are on my skin. Sometimes touch feels good and sometimes touch bothers me or hurts my skin. Sometimes hugs are nice, but other times they feel uncomfortable. Many children with autism are bothered by certain kinds of touch. Or, they might want to feel a certain kind of touch a lot.

I will ~~cross out~~ what **I do not like,** and I will (circle) **what I do like.** Some things might be crossed out *and* circled!

- ▶ shirts and sleeves
- ▶ seams or tags
- ▶ zippers or waistbands
- ▶ socks, seams at the toes
- ▶ shorts and long pants
- ▶ underwear
- ▶ slips, dresses, skirts
- ▶ hats, caps, stocking caps
- ▶ headbands, scarves, hoods
- ▶ silk, denim, cotton, flannel
- ▶ velvet, wool, rayon, polyester
- ▶ necklaces and other jewelry
- ▶ someone kissing me
- ▶ taking a shower
- ▶ taking a bath

- ▶ swimming
- ▶ brushing my hair
- ▶ shampooing my hair
- ▶ cutting my hair
- ▶ people hugging me
- ▶ people bumping me
- ▶ being tapped on the shoulder
- ▶ soft, light touch
- ▶ someone tickling me
- ▶ firm, deep touch, massage
- ▶ someone holding my hand
- ▶ doctors or nurses touching me
- ▶ unexpected touch
- ▶ other: _____

Smelling

Smelling is how people are aware of the world through their noses. Everything in the world has a smell.

Once in a while, children notice strong smells like flowers, or the air after it rains, or a scented candle, or freshly baked bread. They say that these things smell good. Once in a while they might notice other strong smells like rotten food or a poopy diaper. They say that those things smell bad. *Usually children aren't very interested in how things smell.*

Many children with autism pay attention to how things smell. If I don't like how something smells, it might be difficult for me to concentrate on something else.

I will (circle) or highlight what is true for me. 🖉

- ▶ Sometimes a particular smell might attract my attention.
- ▶ I notice how many things smell.
- ▶ I often pick things up to smell them.
- ▶ I might like to smell people's hair or their skin.
- ▶ Other: _____

I like the way these things smell: _____

_____ .

I do not like the way these things smell: _____

_____ .

Seeing

Seeing is what people do with their eyes. Many children with autism see things that other people don't notice. Some children with autism *really like* to watch or look at certain things.

I will (circle) or highlight what is true for me. ✏

I like:

▶ Watching things that are spinning (like ceiling fans).

▶ Looking at things that are stacked or lined up.

▶ Watching things that are flipping (like pages of a book).

▶ Looking at things from out of the corner of my eye.

▶ Holding my fingers and hands in different positions.

▶ Staring at my favorite things, for a long time.

▶ Looking at things that have a certain shape or color.

▶ Looking at bright lights.

▶ other: _____

Some children with autism can get confused or anxious when there are *too many things* to see at the same time.

Places in my life where there are too many things to see at the same time are: _____

_____

_____ .

Tasting

Tasting is what I do when I eat or drink something. Everyone has favorite foods and foods that they don't like.

In addition to taste, some children with autism consider the color or feel of food to be very important. Some children with autism would rather drink than eat. Some children with autism like to taste things that aren't food. They might put paper or toys or other things in their mouths. Some children with autism want to eat the *same thing* for every meal, every day. If that is true, parents might say that a child is a *picky eater*.

I will mark the things that are important to me about food. 🖉

- ▶ The texture of food; how it feels in my mouth
- ▶ The flavor of food; how it tastes
- ▶ The color of the food
- ▶ Wanting to eat the same food every day
- ▶ Wanting to taste different foods, trying new things✳
- ▶ other: _____

✳When my parent says *"Just taste it"* or *"Just try it"* or *"Just take a little bite"* it means that I just have **to take one bite and then chew and swallow it.** When that swallow is finished, I do not have to take another bite of that food during that meal, unless I want to.

Pain

Pain is what people feel when they have been hurt. Most people feel pain when they get injured. Sometimes, people feel pain when they are sick.

When most children feel pain, they automatically stop what they are doing and get help right away. But some children with autism **might not feel** if they are sick or hurt. They might not know when they need help. They might be **so focused** on something that they do not realize when they have been injured. Other children with autism feel **too much pain.** Little things might hurt a lot. **Examples of things that can cause pain are:**

- Touching a hot burner on the stove
- Falling down
- Dropping something heavy on my foot
- Eating food that is too hot
- A door closing on my fingers
- Getting cut and bleeding
- Water that is too hot or too cold
- A sore throat or a fever
- A headache or a stomach ache
- Bare hands in cold weather without mittens

I will circle or highlight what is true for me.

- ▶ I rarely feel pain. I might be injured and not notice.
- ▶ I am very sensitive to pain. Many things hurt me a lot.

The Sensory Experience

Movements

Everyone moves. Many children with autism move their bodies in particular ways. **I will mark the kinds of movements that I sometimes do.** ✏️

- ▶ Flapping my hands
- ▶ Jumping up and down
- ▶ Rocking back and forth
- ▶ Spinning around
- ▶ Pacing back and forth
- ▶ Wiggling fingers or holding my fingers in different positions
- ▶ Flicking my fingers and hands
- ▶ Other: _____

Children who do not have autism might move in these ways, but not as often as I do. *There are reasons for my movements.* I move in those ways when:

- ▶ I am excited and feeling happy.
- ▶ I am excited from feeling anxious or confused.
- ▶ I am bored. I don't have anything else to do.
- ▶ I am anxious. Moving helps me relax and feel better.
- ▶ I am just doing it out of habit - I have done it for a long time.
- ▶ other: _____

The Sensory Experience

Times and Places for Movements

Most children my age do not move like I do. They do not flap their hands or rock or spin around very often. My **movements** might bother teachers and children and parents. It might bother them because it makes me look different from the other children, and they worry that children will make fun of me.

- •I can try to remember to do these movements when I am in a **room by myself.** Maybe I can wait until I am home to move my body in those ways.

If I feel like I have to do these things more often, my parent or teacher or therapist can help me know when and where:

- •They can give me **time** for swinging or for using other therapy equipment.
- •They can teach me **other ways of moving** my body that I might like, too. For example, I might like to rock in a rocking chair or jump on a pogo stick.
- •They can give me a regular time for these and other **exercises.** *(see Chapter 11)*

When other children and adults learn about autism, it won't bother them so much to see my movements. *If they had autism, they probably would move in these ways too.*

The Sensory Experience

For Parents and Teachers

"...everything through the senses seems to come through unfiltered. The finest little detail of something is there whether I want to pay attention to it or not. There's all this information coming in all of the time. Noticing little motions on the side of my field of vision, seeing great levels of details on something that I'm not really looking at, hearing lots of things all at once, noticing the feel of my clothes...

From what I understand, ordinarily most folks don't pay that much attention to all that...as though it doesn't really reach their conscious awareness. But those filters are not there for me. I'm getting all of this data all the time, whether I want it or not.

You've seen the acts in circuses when somebody with a bunch of long thin sticks and a bunch of plates holds them up and spins them, and they run around, seeing how many they can get going all at once? Dealing with everything in life, not just sensory stuff, is like having a bunch of plates going all at once. And when the sensory stuff comes in unfiltered, that means that there are even more plates to take care of.

I've noticed that if I'm under stress, I'll have problems with sensory stuff that is ordinarily OK for me, like a sudden noise that I usually would not respond to. If I'm really stressed, I'd have to wince or cringe. Or a touch that ordinarily would be OK, if I'm real stressed, I'll pull away from it.

So my responses to sensory things are not constant, not the same way all the time. It's just that there is a lot of information, and sometimes I can deal with it, and sometimes I can't."

–Dave Spicer
during a discussion about sensory responses

Ideas in This Chapter

✓ The quiet area

✓ Reducing visual stimulation

✓ Managing auditory stimulation

✓ Controlling tactile stimulation

✓ Smells

✓ The need for oral stimulation

✓ Eating

✓ Visual preferences

✓ Movement for sensory input

✓ Sensory integration evaluation

The quiet area

Give your child the time and place in which to retreat, relax, and recover from sensory overload. Designate a room, or a special area of a room, to sit away from the hustle and bustle. Refer to it as the *quiet area*. Respect the quiet area as a sanctuary for your child, and schedule an adequate number of *quiet area times* during the day. Teach him to go to the quiet area before "it gets to be too much."

Outside, a playhouse, tree house, or a special place in the yard might appeal to some children. One family created a quiet area for their child in a camper, parked in the backyard of their home. John Engle, an adult with autism, once explained that as a child, he used to climb trees, and later in college, he would sit on rooftops. He explained that he discovered at an early age that most people didn't look up, so he was almost always guaranteed a reprieve from the sensory and social demands he found overwhelming.

Reducing visual stimulation

Many adults with autism have said that *night* is their favorite time. The peace and quiet, the reduced visual stimulation, and the fact that most people are asleep, create a wonderfully soothing time in which to read, work, walk, or just sit. Maria White, an adult with autism, has said that she becomes more "alert and energized" when the sun goes down. A darkened room or one with soft lighting may be helpful in preventing or recovering from overstimulation. Cleared or empty space may be more relaxing for some children than a room with lots of clutter. Some individuals have discovered that wearing sunglasses helps.

Managing auditory stimulation

Respect the child's auditory responses to the environment and let him experiment with wearing ear plugs or headphones when necessary. Carpeting and drapery in rooms help to absorb sounds. Prepare your child for noises that can be predicted. For example, let him know ahead of time when the lawn mower or the chain saw will be running. At school, talk to the principal about letting your child know when there will be a fire drill. Listening to favorite music or books on tape may help to soothe and distract from other, less appealing, sounds.

Controlling tactile stimulation

Allow him to choose which clothing to wear to prevent unnecessary discomfort, distraction, or distress. Many adults with autism have said that they prefer to buy two or three duplicates of the same outfits. This way, there is less variation in how the clothing feels from day to day, as well as decreasing the amount of choices they must encounter first thing in the morning when dressing!

Experiment with different types of physical touch and identify which are soothing, calming, or comforting. Schedule time for deep-pressure massage, if indicated. One woman with autism has said that even though it can be uncomfortable to receive a therapeutic massage, she benefits greatly from *giving* them. The repetitive movement and the deep pressure against the palms of her hands helps her relax and feel calmer. A family pet–dog, cat, rabbit, or guinea pig–may be perfect to help soothe your child, although the decision to have a pet for your child must be made carefully; pets are not necessarily appropriate for all children (and all children are not necessarily appropriate for pets!)

Smells

Many children are especially sensitive to smells that are not typically considered offensive, like deodorant, perfume, and hand lotion. Some scents might cause a child to be very uncomfortable, distracted, or upset. Some children become very active and "hyper" when they smell certain scents. Become aware of what odors might be aversive to your child. On the other hand, there may be certain scents that are especially soothing to him. Some families might want to explore the possible benefits of "aromatherapy"—the therapeutic uses of oil essences.

The need for oral stimulation

Allowing the child to chew gum in school may provide the oral stimulation that he needs rather than fighting (a losing battle) with him about chewing the neckline or sleeves of his shirt.

Eating

Your child, like many other children with autism, may be a picky eater. There are some children who only eat crunchy foods, or smooth foods, or certain-colored foods, or a certain brand of a particular food. There often seems to be a particular sensitivity related to the texture. John Engle has said that if left alone, he will eat the same thing every day for long periods of time, especially when he is experiencing a lot of stress. He explains that for him,

> *"...there is so much sensory stimulation in daily life that cannot be avoided, that eating the same thing for all my meals is one way of controlling the overwhelming amount of sensory input I have to deal with."*

John goes on to explain that when he is more relaxed and not as anxious, he is more able to enjoy a larger variety of food.

Your child may be one who eats a variety of food, so this is not an issue. Or, you may struggle with his refusals on a day-to-day basis. You might try introducing *only one* new food at a time, instead of a variety of different foods every day. Make only one new food availabe for "trying" and keep introducing the same one over a period of time. As he grows more familiar with this one new food, he may be willing to try it and eventually learn to enjoy it. Try introducing it at different times of the day, however, so he won't develop a routine of rejecting it every time he sits down for dinner.

Some parents and teachers have been successful with expanding their child's limited diet by using the routine of the *work system (Chapter 9)*. Once your child has learned the routine of following a work system, then you can use the same principal to help him learn to "take a bite" or "eat one spoonful" by showing him a sequence of food on the table. Place a small bites of foods, each on their own spoon or small plate, next to each other in a line, going left-to-right. Alternate the new food with favorite food. In this way, it is absolutely clear to him what to expect, because *he can see* exactly *how much* of the new food he is to eat, *when he is finished* with the new food, and *what comes next*. Start with only one bite of a new food, followed by his favorite food, expanding the sequence later, after he is used to this. If your child is well-versed in following a work system at school or at home, then using the same strategy at meal-time may work. The familiar routine of the work system may help to "overide" the previously-established food routines.

There is more discussion about food and diet in Chapter 11.

Visual preferences

Introduce and teach activities or hobbies that appeal to your child's compelling sensory needs or visual preferences like spinning, flipping, or lining things up. Hobbies that satisfy sensory and visual interests might reduce unusual repetitive behavior, as well as increase leisure skills. Examples are Spin Art, board games with spinners, "Flippin' Flap Jacks," and Solitaire, Rummy, Dominoes, or other games that require lining up and putting things in order. Look for board games that can be adapted for solitary use or simplified for social use. Other ideas are paint-by-number, needlepoint, beading, rug hooking, knitting, crocheting, and other crafts.

Movement for sensory input

Introduce socially acceptable activities which provide sensations similar to his stereotypic movements (as covered in the previous workbook pages about body movements). Sitting in a rocking chair or bouncing on a mini-trampoline are examples of "substitute" movements. According to the natural preferences and needs of your child, include times for swinging, running, Sit 'n' Spins, scooter boards, trampoline, and playing on other equipment. You can also provide locations and times on his schedule when it is OK for his "unique" body movements.

Additional suggestions about physical activity and exercise in your child's daily schedule are covered in Chapter 11 on pages 255 and 267.

Sensory integration evaluation

Evaluation and consultation by an occupational therapist experienced in sensory integration therapy may be helpful. The therapist can give you specific ideas for movement or sensory input based on your child's sensory needs.

Chapter 4: Artistic Talent

Workbook

"John Engle playing his fiddle"

Drawing by Maria White, 1999
Age 21

Drawing and Painting

Drawing and painting are talents that are admired by many people. Drawings and paintings add to the beauty and enjoyment of life.

Many children with autism are quite skilled at drawing and painting. *Maybe they are good artists because they see the details and remember what they see.* Maybe they are visual thinkers who automatically see pictures in their minds. Maybe it is more natural for them to draw or paint, than to express themselves in words.

I will ⬭circle⬭ or highlight what is true for me. 🖉

- ▶ I do not like to draw or paint or other artwork. If I marked this sentence, then I am finished with this page.

- ▶ I like to **draw** or **paint**. (Circle which)

- ▶ I like doing computer graphics.

- ▶ I like _____ (Type of artwork.)

- ▶ It's OK if people want to see my artwork.

- ▶ I don't want people to see my artwork.

- ▶ I would like to go to art classes.

- ▶ I would like to learn how to _____ .

- ▶ I enjoy **looking** at art by other artists. My favorite artists are: _____ .

Music

Most people like to listen to **music**. Some people can express themselves more easily when they make music than when they use words.

Most children with autism enjoy listening to music. Some children with autism have perfect pitch and a natural ability to sing or play a musical instrument.

Maybe children with autism who are musically talented are children with very sensitive hearing.

I will (circle) or highlight what is true for me. 🖉

- ▶ I do not like to sing or to play an instrument. If I marked this, then I do not have to read any more on this page.

- ▶ I like to sing.

- ▶ I like to play a musical instrument (or many instruments). I play the _____ .

- ▶ I like to make music or to sing when I am by myself.

- ▶ I like playing alone, but it is OK if others listen to me.

- ▶ I would like to play an instrument or sing with other people in a chorus, a band, or an orchestra. (Circle which.)

- ▶ I would like to take music lessons or singing lessons.

- ▶ I would like to learn how to _____ .

- ▶ I enjoy listening to music. I like (kinds of music) _____
_____ .

Writing

Literary art includes stories, essays, poetry, and letters. **Writing** can help the writers and the people who read their writing, think clearly, appreciate beauty in the world, laugh, cry, dream, and imagine new things.

Some children with high functioning autism or Asperger Syndrome enjoy words and have a larger vocabulary than most children their age. Some children with high functioning autism or Asperger Syndrome are talented writers.

I will (circle) or highlight what is true for me.

▶ I do not like to write. If I marked this sentence, then I do not have to read any more on this page.

▶ I like to write. I like to write poetry, essays, stories, letters, or email. (Circle which.)

▶ I prefer to keep my writing to myself. I do not like others to read what I have written.

▶ I like other people to read what I have written.

▶ I like to read aloud while other people listen to me.

▶ I would like to write about _____ .

▶ I like to read about _____ .

▶ Other: _____ .

Drama

Drama is an art form that many people enjoy. Many people like to go to the movies, plays, and musicals.

Actors must pretend that they are someone else. Some children with high functioning autism or Asperger Syndrome enjoy acting. *They might be skilled at observing and copying how people move and how they sound.* They like to pretend that they are different characters.

I will (circle) or highlight what is true for me.

- ▶ I am not interested in drama. If I marked this sentence, then I do not need to read any more on this page.
- ▶ I like to imitate the way people move and talk.
- ▶ I like to pretend that I am someone else.
- ▶ Memorizing and remembering my lines is fun.
- ▶ I like to learn different ways to act.
- ▶ I like to dance.
- ▶ I would like to learn more about _____ .
- ▶ I enjoy attending plays, musicals, and/or ballets. My favorites are _____ .

Mechanical Ability

Mechanical ability is usually not often thought of as an artistic talent, although many people who have **mechanical ability** are very creative and talented.

Many children with autism have good mechanical ability. *These children see how things fit together and they like to take things apart, assemble and construct things. They like discovering how things work.*

I will circle or highlight what is true for me. ✎

- ▶ I like taking things apart.
- ▶ I like seeing how things fit together.
- ▶ I like figuring out how things work.
- ▶ I like building and constructing things.
- ▶ I like planning and designing things to build.
- ▶ I am not interested in mechanical things.

I would like to learn more about: (Circle)

Cars	Trains	Heating systems
Carpentry	Construction	Plumbing systems
Electrical systems	Electrical appliances	Computers

Other: _____

Computers

Working with **computers** is usually not thought of as an artistic talent, although many people who are good with computers are very creative and talented.

Many children with autism have excellent skills on computers. *Computers are literal, concrete, and predictable. A computer program follow its rules, exactly.* Using the computer might come naturally and easily to children with autism. There are many different ways that children can enjoy using the computer.

I will (circle) or highlight what is true for me. 🖉

- ▶ I am not especially interested in computers. If I checked this, then I do not have to read any more on this page.
- ▶ I like playing computer games.
- ▶ I like to use the computer to write.
- ▶ I like to use the computer to send and receive e-mails.
- ▶ I like to visit different Web sites on the Internet.
- ▶ I like drawing and designing graphics on the computer.
- ▶ I like programming computers. (Programming is using the language of the computer to make it do things.)
- ▶ I would like to learn how to _____ .
- ▶ Other: _____ .
  .

For Parents and Teachers

Dave Spicer, who is quoted several times in this book, is a talented poet and essayist, however his talent was not noticed or encouraged as a child. He recalls that even though his highest SAT scores were in the *verbal* sections, he was guided to study engineering in college. Dave only became aware of his own creativity with words later; one day, Dave says, a poem just "jumped out" of him.

I asked Dave to think about the questions listed below and to share his thoughts. Many thanks to Dave for pondering this subject and writing this section for parents and teachers.

Ideas in This Chapter

✓ Why do you think artistic expression is important?

✓ What are ways that parents might encourage their child's talent?

✓ Do you have any other insights about persons with autism and talent?

✓ What is your personal experience of developing your talent?

Why do you think that artistic expression is important?

Artistic expression can serve a number of purposes for an autistic person: It can be physically pleasurable, due to the motor or sensory aspects of the activity. These could include the feel or smell of the materials being used, their colors, the sounds made by using them, and so on.

It can be intellectually pleasurable, as the patterns, rhythm, and harmony being externally manifested bring a greater sense of order and balance to one's thoughts.

It can offer practice at self-expression, at having one's thoughts and feelings take form in a way that affect the outside world. This is useful since the very concept of being able to influence the outside world may be foreign.

Particularly with feelings, it can be way of "doing something" with them, and perhaps of "taming" them so they are less overwhelming to experience.

It can be a means of communication. The activity can serve as a kind of bridge connecting one's internal state with the external world. Some autistic people may not realize that it is even possible for this to happen, and so may never expect to be understood. Others may expect everyone to know all their thoughts automatically, and so do not understand that thoughts have to be communicated at all. Using artistic expression as a way to practice communication can help to find the middle ground between these extremes.

It can be a way of interacting with society and contributing to it. The viewpoints of those "outside the mainstream" can offer information and perspective which are not easily available from within it. Systems function much better with feedback, and the impressions of autistic folks, as expressed through art, can help provide this. One result of this feedback can be a broader understanding of the term "society", so that those outside the mainstream are recognized as still being part of it. This in turn brings greater richness through diversity.

What are ways that parents might encourage their child's talent?

A starting point can be the recognition of what is already taking place. It has been suggested that one's very life can be viewed as a canvas upon which one "paints" by living it; with this as a guide, examples of creative expression are likely already present. A child's special interests can offer situations for using artistic talent. How many different ways can the object (or objects) of interest be represented? What different situations can they be represented in? Could there be stories or songs about them? How about "documentaries" or advertising?

Do you have any other insights about persons with autism and talent?

The amount of enjoyment an autistic person gets from an activity may not be evident from his/her demeanor or behavior. Intense absorption may look like dispassionate detachment, and strong feelings of pleasure may be tightly contained within oneself to keep them manageable. Because of this, it may take considerable time to learn what a child is actually interested in and enjoys. If a number of choices are made available, some might be ignored for a long time then suddenly taken up with great enthusiasm. Conversely, a longtime favorite might be suddenly dropped without explanation.

While a parent may very much want to learn why this happens, the child may well be unable to communicate or even understand the reasons. It may be quite frustrating to have a child who acts and speaks very precisely, explaining some of his or her preferences and actions in detail, being unable to answer a direct question about others.

The area of artistic expression does not appear to be entirely rational, which can cause difficulty to those who seek logical understanding of things. Drawings, songs, poems, and the like can seem to appear "out of nowhere" for no apparent reason. This may be disquieting to the person creating them, perhaps causing a blend of simultaneous enjoyment and apprehension. On the other hand, if the creation is in response to strong feelings like frustration or anger, matters of intellectual appreciation may be completely set aside as the process becomes almost a visceral one.

What is your personal experience of developing your talent?

My own experience with creative expression is that of pent-up energy seeking an outlet. This energy is intensified by enjoying the creative expression of others. I do not feel this energy can be created, but rather that people can seek to become conduits for it. My challenges in this area do not involve trying to "become more creative", but rather to remove the barriers which keep what I have inside me from being expressed more freely.

I am grateful that I do not have to completely understand the process of "creative expression" to be able to use it. As an autistic person, there are some aspects of life which, even though they escape my full understanding, I can still participate in and enjoy.

Contributed by Dave Spicer 1999

Chapter 5: People

Workbook

Drawings by Brian Davis, 1998, age 14
Paul Hoyt, 1999, age 13
Thomas Johnson, 1994, age 5; 1999, age 10

People

People are a part of life. There are people at home and people at school. There are children, teenagers, adults, and elderly people. There are people in stores, in cars, and people walking. Sometimes they are alone and sometimes they are in groups.

People are different from **objects**. *Objects* are things like furniture, toys, and rocks. *Objects* stay the same unless you do something to them. **Some objects in my life are:**

1 _____   3 _____

2 _____   4 _____

People change. It is hard to know what will happen with people. Sometimes they talk loud. Sometimes they talk softly. Sometimes they laugh. Sometimes they are quiet. Sometimes they look at me and sometimes they look away. The same person can look different from before. *Voices change, faces and hair change, clothes change, and movements change.*

I never know when a person will be different than before. People can be unpredictable and puzzling. Sometimes I like being with people and sometimes I prefer being alone.

I get confused when people _____

_____ .

The People in My Family

Most children live with their families. Some children live with one parent. Some children live with two parents. Some children have step-parents. My **parents'** names are:

1 _____   4 _____

2 _____   5 _____

3 _____   6 _____

Some children have brothers and sisters. I might have brothers and sisters. If I do, the names of my **brothers and sisters** are:

1 _____   5 _____

2 _____   6 _____

3 _____   7 _____

4 _____   8 _____

Sometimes, grandparents or aunts or uncles or cousins or friends live together in the same house. If **other people** live with me, their names are:

1 _____   3 _____

2 _____   4 _____

*More on **people in my family...***

Some children have two families. This happens when their parents are separated or divorced. Or, a child might have two or even three families if he or she lives with a foster family.

I will (circle) or highlight what is true for me. ✏

- ▶ I have one family. We all live together in one home.
- ▶ I have two families, in two different homes.
- ▶ I have three families, in three different homes.
- ▶ My parents live together.
- ▶ My parents live in separate homes.
- ▶ My parents are divorced. They live in different homes.
- ▶ One of my parents has **remarried**∗.
- ▶ Both of my parents have remarried.
- ▶ I have a step-mother. She is my father's wife.
- ▶ I have a step-father. He is my mother's husband.
- ▶ I have half-brothers or **half-sisters**∗∗.
- ▶ I have step-brothers or **step-sisters**∗∗∗.
- ▶ other: _____

∗**Remarried** means that my parent is now married to a new person. This new person is my step-parent (step-mother or step-father).

∗∗**Half-brothers** and **half-sisters** are siblings whose parents are my parent and my step-parent.

∗∗∗**Step-brothers** and **step-sisters** are siblings who were born when my step-parent was married to someone else, before.

New or Different People at Home

Sometimes **people** come to my home for a visit. Some visits are short, but others might last a few days, or weeks. Special new people might move in and live with us.

It might take time for me to get used to changes at home. **I will mark the events that have happened at home.** 🖉

- ▶ Having company or visitors
- ▶ Holidays when grandparents, aunts, uncles, or cousins visit
- ▶ Family parties, birthday parties
- ▶ Friends of brothers or sisters coming to play
- ▶ My friends coming to play
- ▶ Men or women coming to repair, build, or paint something
- ▶ One or both parents going out of town
- ▶ Babysitters
- ▶ A new baby
- ▶ Moving to a new neighborhood
- ▶ Parents who live in different houses
- ▶ Parents that are divorced
- ▶ My divorced parents getting married to someone else
- ▶ A new step-parent
- ▶ New step-sisters or step-brothers
- ▶ Other: _____
- ▶ Other: _____

My Family Tree

A **family tree** is a diagram of a family. It is called a family *tree* because it shows how the people are connected to each other, like branches and stems of a tree growing out from the trunk. My *family tree* shows how I am connected to my family.

My parent and I can fill it out the family tree on the next page by following these directions. We will check ☑ each box as we do what it says.

☐ 1. Start at the bottom by writing my name on the line.

☐ 2. Write in the names of my mother and father. If I have stepparents, I will write their names in, too.

☐ 3. Write in the names of my brothers and sisters on the dotted lines going down.

☐ 4. Write the names of my grandparents at the top.

☐ 5. Write the name of my aunts and uncles on the lines going down from my grandparents.

☐ 6. If I want to include my cousins, then I need to draw lines coming out from their parents (my aunts and uncles).

☐ 7. When finished, I can show it to someone in my family.

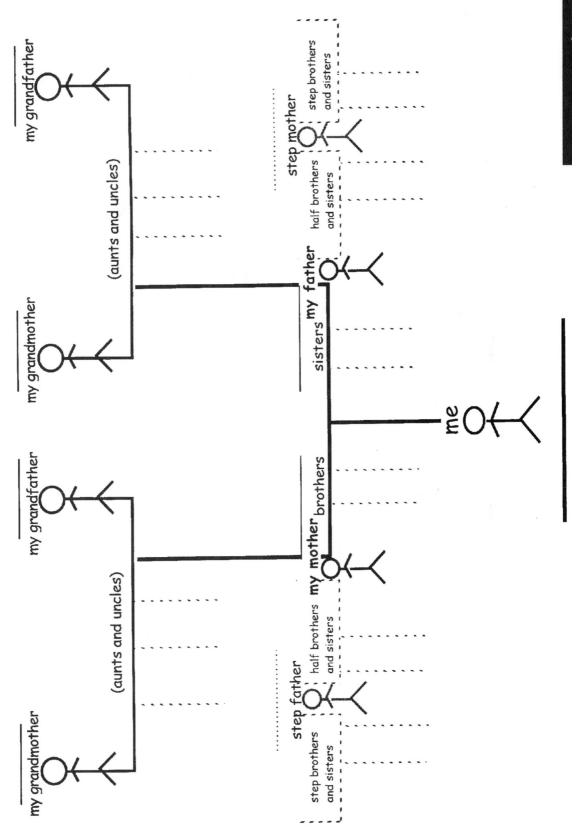

New or Different People at School

Sometimes **new or different people** come into my classroom. Many children are happy to have new teachers and new students in the class. They think it is fun. But children with autism might become anxious, worried, scared, or angry when there are changes with people at school. It is unfamiliar and different.

It may take more time for me to get used to new people at school. **I will mark what bothers me at school:** 🖉

▶ Substitute teachers

▶ Student teacher

▶ New teacher or assistant

▶ Therapists coming to the classroom

▶ When the teacher moves my desk

▶ When other children's desks are moved

▶ My parents coming to my classroom

▶ Special visitors to the classroom

▶ Different children standing next to me in line

▶ Different children sitting next to me at lunch

▶ Different children playing on the playground

▶ A new student in my class

▶ Me going to a new class

▶ Other: _____

▶ Other: _____

▶ Other: _____

Other Important People

There are **other important people** in my life. At school, the important adults are the ones I talk to every day. They might be teachers, assistants, therapists, the principal, office workers, cooks, and custodians. The names of the **important adults for me at school** are:

1 _____ 4 _____

2 _____ 5 _____

3 _____ 6 _____

There are *children* who are important to me at school. They might be **friends and helpers**. Their names are:

1 _____ 4 _____

2 _____ 5 _____

3 _____ 6 _____

There might be *other* important people in my life, too. They might be friends of my family, people at church or temple, at my parent's work, and at other places. Other important people in my life are:

1 _____ 3 _____

2 _____ 4 _____

People

Paying Attention to More Than One Person

Most children who have two parents have a relationship with both of their parents, and maybe relationships with other adults, like grandparents or aunts and uncles. In school, most students listen to and pay attention to more than one teacher.

Children with autism sometimes get confused when they are supposed to pay attention to more than one person. Often, it is easier and more natural for a child with autism to rely on just one person. *That is why some children with autism might listen to one parent and ignore the other parent.* Sometimes the other parent feels left out. **I will mark what is true for me.** 🖉

▶ I usually pay attention to my mother *and* my father. I talk and listen to **both** of them.

▶ I usually just pay attention to **only one** of my parents. I mostly listen to my _____.

▶ I live with one parent, or just one parent at a time.

▶ I pay attention to **all** of my teachers. There are ___.(number?)

▶ I usually pay attention to **only one** of my teachers at school. I mostly listen to _____ (name).

▶ There are many adults who care about me, and I would like to have relationships with **more** of them. I would like to become more familiar with _____ (name).

▶ There are many adults who care about me, but right now, I would rather have a relationship with **only one** adult at school, and **one** adult at home.

Being Safe

Most people in the world are good people. Good people are usually kind and helpful. I am **safe** with them.

But there are some people who are not good. There are a few children and adults who might try to hurt others or make them do things that are wrong. Someone might act kind, but he or she might not be a good person.

It can be difficult for many children to know if someone is a safe person or not. But it is especially hard for children with autism to know if someone is safe. *Some children with autism try to do what someone tells them to do, even if they don't understand why.* Or, they might be very fearful and think that everyone wants to hurt them, even if someone is really a good and safe person.

I will (circle) or highlight what is true for me. 🖉

- ▶ Everyone is my friend.
- ▶ I always try to do what someone tells me to do, even if I do not understand why.
- ▶ I am afraid of people I do not know.
- ▶ Even when my parent says that it's OK, I am *still* afraid of new people.
- ▶ I wonder if _____ (name) is a safe person?
- ▶ There are children at school who tell me to do things, and I do not understand why. Sometimes I might feel afraid or confused. The children tell me to _____

  _____ .

*More on **being safe...***

Most children at school are nice. But there are a few children who are not nice. There might be a child at school or in my neighborhood who acts like a *bully*.

A child who acts like a bully tells me to do things that are wrong or bad or scary. Sometimes he or she tries to scare or hurt other children. He or she might hit or beat up someone. A child who acts like a bully might pretend to be nice, but then does something mean. It is hard to understand why these children do what they do.

If there is a child who does things that scare me or does things that I do not understand, I must tell an adult. I must tell my teacher or my parent or another adult what the child does.

- I can keep myself safe by telling my parent or teacher or other adult when there is something that I do not understand.

- The adults will only be able to help me if I tell them what has happened. If I do not tell them, then they will not know what has happened, and they will not be able to help me.

- It is good to tell my parent or teachers when I do not understand something about a child. I do not understand why_____

_____.

*More on **being safe**...*

My parent or teacher can make a list of some of the special people in my life who can help me. Some are adults and some are children. These are the people who I will tell when I need help or when I do not understand something. **Here is a list of the children and adults who can help me:**

1 _____   4 _____

2 _____   5 _____

3 _____   6 _____

My parent and I can do these things to help me learn how to be safe:

- •My parent or teacher can make me an ***ID card*** with my phone number and address to keep with me. Other important names and phone numbers might be on the card too.

- • I can *practice* using different types of telephones, including pay phones.

- • My parent can write on the back of the ***ID card***, what I need to say, so I can read the words to say if I ever need to call for help.

- • I can *practice* calling the phone numbers and talking to the people on my ***ID card***.

For Parents and Teachers

"People bothered me. I didn't know what they were for or what they would do to me. They were not always the same and I had no security with them at all. Even a person who was always nice to me might be different sometimes. Things didn't fit together for me with people. Even when I saw them a lot, they were still in pieces, and I couldn't connect them to anything."

–Sean Barron, from
There's A Boy In Here, by Sean and Judy Barron
published by Simon & Schuster

Consider using visually structured strategies to prepare your child for social events and to clarify relationships with the people in her life. Although these ideas may not magically or instantly change the underlying mystery regarding "people," structured strategies may help to ease some of the confusion by adding predictability, familiarity, and a sense of order.

Ideas in This Chapter

✓ List *new people* on the schedule

✓ Use a calendar

✓ Write a *schedule of events* when waiting for visitors

✓ Overnight visitors

✓ Parents out of town

✓ Changes in the family structure

✓ Substitute teachers

✓ Social stories

✓ Teach a routine for *getting help* in public

List *new people* on the schedule

When there will be a change from the usual people at home or at school, you can write it on your child's daily schedule. Write the new person's name alongside the appropriate entry, even if your child doesn't yet know who the person is. By routinely seeing new people indicated on her schedule, your child will come to handle such changes with less anxiety. Developing a routine *of seeing new people on the schedule* not only clarifies the change, but gives it added meaning. Remember that to a child who relies on routines, the routine *itself* becomes meaningful.

A short written explanation at the top of the schedule might also be reassuring. For example, a note to prepare a child for a new sitter might read,

> Debbie is sick. She has to stay at her house on Coleman Street today. Ms. Hunter will babysit from 4:00 - 7:00.

Use a calendar

Give your child her own calendar. Write what will be coming up on the appropriate day's square and point it out to her ahead of time. Attach the new person's photograph to the calendar for more specific visual information.

Use the calendar to prepare your child for physical changes on familiar people, such as new glasses, contacts, haircuts, and vacation tans. Mark the calendar when you or a significant person will come home with a new or changed appearance.

A few children become overly focused on an upcoming event when they see it indicated on the calendar. For some, seeing the event listed on the calendar can be anxiety-provoking. Difficulty understanding the passage of time can make this problem worse. They may think that the event is going to happen immediately. You will need to notice how much preparation time works best for your child. It may be that one day's notice is better than a week's notice. As your child gains more experience with the calendar, using it may prove to be more helpful in the long run, even if it causes problems at first.

In order to help her learn and understand the concept of the calendar, have your child mark off each day on the calendar before bed, and circle the square for "today" each morning. This routine may help her learn more about the passage of time from day to day.

Write a *schedule of events* when waiting for visitors

Prepare for visitors coming to your home by making a checklist of the things your child will do during the visit. List some activities which allow her to play by herself. List some activities which include the visitor, if appropriate.

Your child will probably be more successful in her social interactions with the visitor if the activities involve her interests, and if the activities have a clear beginning and end. Examples of the types of social activities that can be structured are: card games or lotto games, Bingo, naming the people and places in a family photo album, and "taking orders" from the visitors for refreshments from a list you have written on a note pad.

Overnight visitors

For overnight visitors, mark the calendar by highlighting the days to show how long the visitor(s) will stay. On the calendar, write something significant that your child will do after the visit is over on that day, so she can see what will happen next.

Remember to include information about the visit on her daily schedule, as well. Next to the appropriate entries, add information that may be significant for her, such as who will sit around the table at dinner time, who will sleep where, and which TV programs might be watched.

Parents out of town

Mark the calendar to show the days when you or your spouse will be out of town. Mark when you will return. On the appropriate calendar square, write where the absent parent will be each day or something concrete that he or she is doing: *Daddy drives to Atlanta, Mommy's at work in the Flat Iron Building, or Daddy visits Aunt Suzie,* and *Daddy comes home.*

Write short letters to be given to your child each day you are out of town. Help her understand that you haven't just disappeared, but that you are somewhere, doing something, and that you will return on a specific date. Date the letters as if you are writing it each day.

Remember to include significant information on her schedule, like when it is time to say goodbye, and which people are going to be involved with her on which days, and what they will do. Help the changes be more predictable. Don't assume that she knows and understands all of the relevant details.

If you have already been using a calendar and a schedule on a regular basis, then the whole process will be more familiar to her and she will handle the changes more easily.

Changes in the family structure

If there are changes or additions to the family because of separation, divorce or remarriage, draw a diagram or a family tree *(see pages 86-87)* so she can see how she and the people are connected and to give a sense of order to the changes. Record births and deaths of important people and pets on the calendar. Write social stories *(see below)* to give more information about these confusing changes.

Allow her to have ample "alone time" or "quiet time" at school and at home.

Substitute teachers

To prepare for school days with substitute teachers, create a file of photographs and/or name cards of substitute teachers. Attach the appropriate photo or name card to the classroom calendar or the student's calendar to show when the substitute is coming.

To prepare for the teacher's absence at the last minute: Have your child look through the substitute teacher photo file once a week so she is familiar with the photographs and names. First thing in the morning when the teacher is absent, she locates the appropriate photo and posts it in the room. If there is no photo, she can post the name card, and later that morning, have her take a Polaroid picture of the new substitute to add to the file.

Social stories

Write a social story about the specific event that cause confusion or stress. A social story, written from the perspective of the child, provides her with accurate information regarding what occurs in a situation, and why. No assumptions are made about what she does or does not understand. Carol Gray has written several articles and books on how to write social stories, as well as collections of sample social stories. For more information on social stories, see page 237 and the *Recommended Resources* at the end of this book.

The following is a social story which was written for a third grade child who had great difficulty every time there was a substitute teacher in his class. Because of personal health issues, Mrs. Smith knew that she was going to be absent many days that winter, and expected that he would have problems. After talking with the student, I discovered that he thought the substitute teacher was like a "walk-in" who just showed up. He did not understand the reason that there was a different person, nor did he understand that this different person was supposed to take his teacher's place.

Substitute Teacher Days

My teacher is Mrs. Smith. Most of the time she is at school on Mondays, Tuesdays, Wednesdays, Thursdays, and Fridays.

Some days are different. Sometimes Mrs. Smith has to stay at her house because she is sick or she has to go to the doctor's office. On those days, she cannot come to school.

The children in our class still need to have a teacher even if Mrs. Smith cannot come to school. On those days, the principal asks a special teacher to be the teacher in our class. This special teacher is called a **substitute teacher** because she is **substituting** for Mrs. Smith. Usually, our substitute teacher is Mrs. Rider, but sometimes it might be someone else.

Mrs. Smith does not always know when she will have to stay at home. The other children and I will find out if we are going to have a substitute teacher when we get to school in the morning.

The substitute teacher looks different than Mrs. Smith, but she says what Mrs. Smith wants her to say. On substitute teacher days I will try to work quietly just like I do when Mrs. Smith is here.

Teach a routine for getting help in public

Maria White, one of the illustrators of this book, uses public transportation every day. She insisted that this book contain information on safety. Have your child carry an ID card, or wear an ID bracelet or necklace.

Create a special ID card with information on both sides. One side of the card can contain the typical identification information. The other side can be a "cue card" for your child to use in an emergency. It might contain reminders like how to use a pay phone or how to ask a store manger to use the phone. The written reminders would augment your teaching her how to make a phone call in public. If the information needed cannot fit on the back of card, make a special small folded card that can fit into a wallet, purse, or a pocket.

Practice using public pay phones. Write and laminate the directions, listing the steps to follow in sequence. As your child becomes familiar with the routine, list the steps on a small card, or the back of her ID card.

Depending on your child and her ability to function independently in this kind of situation, you may want to teach her to give the cue card to a store manager for help. It may be easier for her to hand a card to a salesperson when she is feeling anxious, than to try to talk. The message on the card might read *"I need help. Can you help me call home?"* Teach her a routine of going into a store, asking for the manager, and asking to use the phone (or handing the cue card). Practice frequently, first at home, and then in different public locations, like the mall, etc. You might feel more comfortable initially setting these up in a familiar store where you are known.

Keep in mind that even though your child may be very verbal, when under stress she may not be able to use her verbal skills effectively. By providing her with an alternate communication system *(a written cue to read or to hand to someone)*, she may be more able to function in an emergency when under stress.

Remember to include practice sessions and list them on her schedule. If she resists your teaching her, *or if you want help with this*, ask another significant adult—a teacher, friend, grandparent, aunt, uncle, or older cousin—to read these suggestions and help set it up.

Chapter 6: Understanding

Workbook

Drawing by Thomas Johnson, 1995
Age 6

Eye Contact

Eye contact means looking directly at someone's eyes. Many children can listen and understand better when they look directly into the eyes of the person who is talking. *Most children make eye contact when they are paying attention.* That is why people think that if I am looking directly at their eyes, I will understand them better. When I look away, they think that I am not paying attention. That is true for many children, *but it is not true for most children who have autism.*

I will ⬭circle⬭ or ▨highlight▨ what is true for me. ✏

- ▶ I can make eye contact *or* I can listen, but it is hard to do both at the same time.

- ▶ It is difficult to understand what the person is saying when I have to look at their eyes.

- ▶ It is easier for me to understand what people are saying when I look somewhere else.

- ▶ I do not like eye contact because it is uncomfortable.

- ▶ Sometimes it is easy to make eye contact and listen at the same time.

- ▶ Other:_____

If someone says *"Look at me"* when they want to get my attention, and if I have difficulty with this, I can say:

I **am** paying attention.
Right now, I can listen better when I look away.

Understanding

Words:
Literal Meanings and Figures of Speech

Some simple words and phrases have two meanings.

The first meaning is literal. **Literal** is when the word means exactly what it says. Most children with autism understand words this way.

But sometimes people use words in another way. They don't mean it literally. These different meanings are called **figures of speech.**

I might be confused by *figures of speech*. I might think about the literal meaning of the words and might not understand what the person means. For example:

- **Hit the road** doesn't really mean to literally hit the road. When people say *hit the road*, it means that *it is time to go somewhere.*

- **Off the wall** doesn't really mean that something is hanging off the wall. When people say *off the wall*, it means that *something is unusual or odd.*

- **Straighten up** doesn't really mean that someone needs to stand straight up. When people say *straighten up*, it means that they want you to *have good behavior and to follow the rules.*

*More Examples of **Figures of Speech...***

Someone can help me list more figures of speech and what they mean.

Understanding

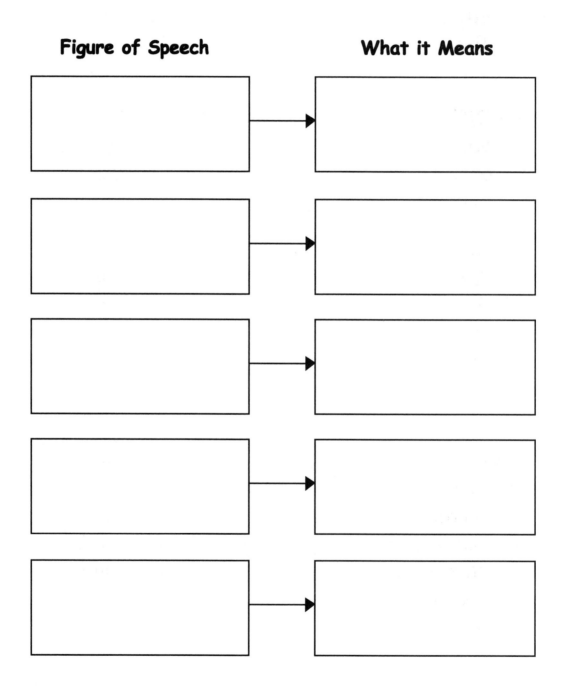

Figure of Speech   **What it Means**

Body Language and Facial Expressions

People communicate by talking and writing. People also communicate by moving their faces and their bodies. When they communicate by moving their bodies, it is called **body language**. When they communicate by moving their faces, it is called using **facial expressions**.

- *Different body language means different things.* For example, when a person turns and puts her back to you, it might mean that she doesn't want to talk anymore.

- *Different facial expressions mean different things.* For example, when a person moves his eyebrows close together making lines in his skin, it might mean that he is confused, or it might mean that he is starting to get angry.

The different meanings of body language and facial expressions are not always exact, but most children understand them easily. *I can see that people move their bodies and faces, but I do not always know what it means.* Body language and facial expressions are difficult for children with autism to understand.

Understanding

*More on **Body Language and Facial Expressions...***

When people want to communicate with me, they should communicate so I know exactly what they mean.

It is best for someone to communicate in *words* that are:

- specific,

- concrete,

- and literal.

If I do not understand what a person is saying, I can say to that person,

"Will you please be more specific?"

*Examples of facial expressions that are **happy**...*

I will look through magazines for pictures of people's faces with **happy** expressions. I will cut out **two** happy expressions and tape them here. ✄

*Examples of facial expressions that are **not happy...***

I can look through magazines for pictures of people's faces with expressions that are **not happy**. I will cut out two, and tape them here. ✂

Understanding

Difficulty Understanding People

When people talk, I can listen to the words. Even though I know the words, *sometimes I don't understand all the words together.*

I will (circle) or highlight what is true for me. 🖉

It is difficult for me to understand, when:

- ▶ People talk quickly.
- ▶ They use too many words.
- ▶ They use words that I don't know.
- ▶ People use *figures of speech.* *(See pages 103-104)*
- ▶ They talk to me when there are too many other noises.
- ▶ They don't wait for me to think about what they have said.
- ▶ People pronounce words differently.
- ▶ People talk with a foreign accent or different dialect.
- ▶ They want me to make eye contact; they say *"look at me"*.
- ▶ They talk to me when I am thinking about something else.
- ▶ People talk to me when I am worried or anxious.
- ▶ other: _____

People in my life who are *difficult* to understand, are:

1 _____   3 _____

2 _____   4 _____

Understanding People Better

Some people are easy to understand. People in my life who I understand *easily* are:

1 _____   3 _____

2 _____   4 _____

I will (circle) or highlight what is true for me. 🖉

I can understand people better when they:

▶ Use fewer words.

▶ Talk at a slower speed.

▶ Pause, and give me time to think and understand.

▶ Remember that I understand words literally.

▶ Talk to me in a quiet place.

▶ Stop to ask if I understand them.

▶ Don't insist on eye contact. It's OK if I look away.

▶ Write the words down, so I can read the words.

▶ other: _____

▶ other: _____

▶ other: _____

Seeing What They Mean

Many children with autism understand people better when they can **see** what is being communicated. It might be easier for me to understand people when I can **read** what they are saying or if they show me **pictures**.

One girl with autism told her teachers,

"I understand when you talk,
*but I **really** understand when you write it down."*

If someone wants to tell me something important, it might help if they write down what they are saying. It might help to have a conversation while sitting next to someone at the computer. The other person can type and talk, and I can read what is being said. Then it can be my turn to talk and type, or I can just talk.

I will mark what I like: ✐

- ▶ When people just talk. I can understand perfectly when I listen to what they are saying.

- ▶ When people just write it down. I can understand better when I read, without having to listen.

- ▶ When people talk *and* write it down. I can understand better when I can listen *and* read what they are saying.

- ▶ When people type their words on a computer while they are talking. I can understand easily when I read and listen while we are sitting at a computer.

- ▶ I don't know what makes it easier for me to understand.

- ▶ other: _____

Tuning Out

Some children with autism might not hear or understand what someone is saying because they **tune out**. When they *tune out* they miss what has been said.

I will (circle) or highlight what is true for me. ✎

- ▶ Sometimes **I tune out.**
- ▶ I **never** tune out.
- ▶ I do not know if I tune out.

Some children *tune out* for only a few seconds; only a very short time. Sometimes they might tune out for a long time. They might miss lots of information. If I tune out, it may be because:

- • I am overwhelmed by too many sights and sounds. Tuning out is like taking a *break*.

- • I might be paying more attention to thoughts and feelings *inside* of me.

- • I tune out because _____ .

The ideas in this book can help me with all the things I have to hear, see, feel, and understand.

Understanding

For Parents and Teachers

"I understand when you talk to me, but I really understand when you write it down."

–Maria White at age 17,
when meeting with her new teachers, the last semester of high school.

Ideas in This Chapter

✓ A critical gap between talking and understanding

✓ Take a close look

✓ The question of eye contact

✓ Choice of words

✓ The way you speak

✓ Be aware of distractions

✓ Structuring time to listen

✓ Body language

✓ Writing it down

✓ Tuning out

A critical gap between talking and understanding

Children with autism frequently have difficulties understanding language and processing auditory information. Typically, their comprehension is weaker, compared to their overall cognitive abilities. Receptive language difficulties are more obvious among children who are nonverbal and those who have significantly limited skills. However, an additional problem emerges for verbal high functioning children with autism.

Your child can talk and read. She may be talented in one or more areas. She might perform well on some standardized tests. She may be quiet or introspective or she may be quite articulate about certain subjects. Some high functioning children with autism are very talkative, and some are known as "little professors." It is no wonder that teachers and parents assume that their high functioning child with autism understands everything that is said.

Frequently though, it is found that the child may demonstrate a critical gap between expressive and receptive language skills. *A complete speech and language evaluation may be indicated, with special focus on receptive language, pragmatics, and the social use of language and communication.*

Take a close look

Even if your child has a large vocabulary, she might have difficulty making sense of all that she hears. So much of her understanding is related to the unique way that she thinks and learns, her focus on particular subjects, how she experiences the sensory environment, and how she interprets social situations.

Can your child digest and organize the large amount of verbal information encountered in school? How does she interpret the concepts, details, nuances, and meaning of everyday conversation?

Examine the manner in which you communicate. Observe your habits and notice your assumptions about communication. Most of us talk automatically, without giving thought to how well the child may be receiving the information. We need to slow down and notice how we use words, how we explain and provide information, the pace of our speech, and our assumptions about what we are communicating *nonverbally.*

As with all the suggestions in this book, you must determine through trial and observation, which of these issues matter most in helping your individual child deepen her understanding.

The question of eye contact

It is a commonly held belief that in order for the listener to understand what the speaker is saying, the listener must be looking at the speaker. Eye contact is an indication that the listener is paying attention. Logic and experience tell us that if the listener is looking elsewhere, it is proof that she is not paying attention. So, in order to make sure that a child is paying attention to his teacher or parent, she must first make eye contact. True?

Not always. It may be true for most neurotypical children, but it is not true for those children who have autism.

Adults with autism speak clearly and plainly about the issue of eye contact. One person said that he can look at someone, *or* listen to someone, but not look and listen at the *same time.* Another very poignantly asks, ***"Do you want me to look at you, or do you want me to understand what you are saying?"*** Yet another person said that he can make eye contact if necessary, but that much of his comprehension is then *"sacrificed."*

"I can actually pay closer attention with my eyes closed."

–John Engle age 31,
when explaining that he was still listening

It appears that the issue is not only an "either/or" situation but that comprehension actually may increase for many children when they are given the freedom to look away in another direction while processing the spoken word. Simultaneously *looking* (attending to and interpreting someone's eyes and facial expression) and *listening* (processing language), while reflecting on the *meaning* and then noticing one's own *response*, is a complicated process which requires that the listener integrate multiple perspectives.

The amount of stimulation and "social expectation" (according to one man with autism) that is present with eye contact can be overwhelming. And a young woman with autism has said that eye contact is sometimes physically painful.

Allow your child to follow her instinctive inclination to look away when she is listening, if that is what comes naturally to her. Acknowledge the fact that she is trying to process what you are saying the best she can. Teach your child about eye contact and how it is perceived by the mainstream, neurotypical culture, but appreciate the differences that autism creates. Respect these differences, and teach other important people in your child's life to respect them also.

Choice of words

Remember that your child's first interpretation of a word will probably be its literal meaning. When you want something to be understood clearly, use words and explanations which are concrete and literal.

After making sure that your child understands what you are saying, you might want to take the opportunity to teach other ways of saying the same thing. It might be fun to make a list of alternative phrases and figures of speech, paired with their literal meanings.

The way you speak

It may take your child longer than anticipated to process verbal information. Remember to pause and wait in silence before expecting a reply. Refrain from repeating yourself, unless she asks. Take a breath, be patient, and remember that your pause may seem like eternity to you, but in reality, it isn't.

Slow down if you have a tendency to talk quickly.

Try to get in the habit of speaking in a calm, matter-of-fact tone of voice, especially when dealing with subjects or situations that may be stressful to your child. Too much emotion in your voice might be distracting or confusing.

Try not to be too wordy. The most effective communication from your child's point of view is one that is concise and simple. She will be able to pay attention to what is most relevant when you limit extraneous information.

Be aware of distractions

Pay attention to the surrounding environment when talking with your child. If there are distractions, your child may not be able to concentrate on what is being said. Wait until later when things calm down, or move to a quieter and calmer place. Say **"Let's go over here..."** or **"Let's move to the other room so we can talk and listen to each other more easily."**

Try to become aware of your child's "inner environment," and notice when she is distracted by her own thoughts or when she is becoming anxious. If she is upset because of something that has happened, or if she is focused on a particular idea or subject, she will not be ready to listen and take in new information.

Structuring time to listen

Use her daily schedule to help her manage her "inner distractions" or her need to talk about her favorite subjects. If something else needs to be done or talked about, or if she needs to let go of a particular subject right now, you can use her schedule to help clarify that it is time to move on and that she can still talk about *her* concern or subject, later. For example:

> Get her schedule while she is watching, and write a new entry showing when it will be time for her to talk about her topic. Point to her schedule while you say, *"First we are talking about [parent's subject] and then it will be time for [feeding the dog] and then it will be time for [her concern or subject.]"* Seeing, concretely, that she will get to talk or engage in "her" subject might allow her to be able to do something else, or to listen to something else you have to say.

Although this example refers to a home situation, the same strategy can be applied at school. Review the ideas on pages 38-42.

There may be times when you agree that it is important to talk about or deal with the subject that is of her immediate concern, right now. Again, use the schedule to clarify what is expected. She needs to see that she cannot talk about it for the rest of the day, that there are other things to do, too. This may even come as a relief to her. Add or change the schedule accordingly. On her schedule in the appropriate spot, you can write *"talk about _____ until _____."* Then, point out on the schedule what will be happening next.

Body language

The interpretation of body language is difficult to teach, because of its transient nature and the fact that subtle changes of movement or posture can result in dramatically different meanings. Individual differences make this area all the more perplexing. Identical postures or movements by one person do not guarantee the same interpretation when done by another person.

One young adult with autism went to the library in search of books that explained body language. He was able to memorize a few basics, although body language and nonverbal communication still remain a mystery to him. In the end, it may simply be enlightening for young people with autism to know that there *is* such a thing as body language, and to realize that it is hard to interpret.

On the other hand, depending on your child and their interest in exploring this complex issue, you might want to point out common gestures, expressions, postures, and stances. Label what you consider to be the most common interpretation of body language basics, especially those that occur on a regular basis in your home or classroom. If appropriate, identify these on you or someone else during the actual act of communication, while it is happening. One young woman has recently learned to ask important people in her life what their body language and facial expressions mean, as they are talking.

If there is sufficient interest, motivation, or need, you might make a game of it, in the style of "charades." Family members or classmates can take turns modeling gestures and postures while others have fun guessing the meaning. When we do this, we will discover just how difficult it can be to define nonverbal communication.

A similar activity can be designed using videotapes of dramatic programs such as soap operas. Pause the tape at the pertinent moments to discuss the possible meaning. Rewind to more closely examine and label the various postures and gestures.

If you want to learn more about this area of communication that most of us take for granted, see the book, **Teaching Your Child the Language of Social Success**, by Duke, Nowicki, and Martin. It is listed in the *Recommended Resources* at the end of this book.

Writing it down

Most children with autism have strong visual skills and they tend to respond positively to instruction that is geared to a visual style of learning. Pictures, symbols, and photographs may enhance comprehension in certain situations with some children, although with the majority of high functioning children with autism, the written word is often most useful.

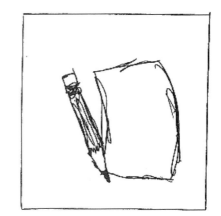

If you want to increase your child's comprehension, *write down* what you are saying as you are speaking to her. Consider doing this, especially when you want to be sure that your child understands the message.

When your child is anxious or upset, you may find that the most effective way to communicate with her is by simply writing her a note. *(See pages 111 and 261.)*

Encourage spontaneous communication by sitting side by side at a computer and typing while you speak. The visual element enhances comprehension, and if you develop a turn-taking game while doing this, conversation skills may increase with practice and familiarity.

Some children can process information more easily if the verbal and the visual are not given simultaneously, but rather one after the other. The sequence may be significant; for some, it may work best if the written word comes first to prepare and help the child focus, followed by the spoken word. For other children, the written word needs to follow the spoken word in order to clarify the meaning. There is more discussion about this in Chapter 8.

It is easier to help your child understand the big picture, like expectations at home and school, when you structure things in visually clear ways. Using a daily schedule has been discussed at length in Chapters 2, 3, and 5.

Additional visually structured teaching strategies such as a work system, written instructions, checklists, rules, and other visual methods to increase your child's understanding at school will be introduced in Chapter 9.

Chapter 11 deals with helping your child understand what happens when she feels upset. Visual stategies such as Mind the Gap and the Emotion-meter may be helpful.

Tuning out

As introduced on page 112 of the workbook, your child's response to an overwhelming environment may be to "tune out". However, most professionals recommend that children with autism be evaluated by a neurologist to rule out other complications. Especially if your child has staring spells, repetitive eye movements, falls asleep in the middle of actitivies, falls asleep often, loses skills that she has mastered, exhibits seizure-like behavior, has had a seizure, or seems to "tune out" often, she should undergo a neurological evaluation.

Chapter 7: Thoughts

Workbook

Drawing by Thomas Johnson, 1999
Age 10

What Are Thoughts?

Thoughts are what I see or hear or feel in my mind...

- when I remember something that has happened,
- when I see a picture in my mind,
- when I remember how something felt, or
- when I think words quietly to myself.

Everyone has thoughts. Thoughts are words or pictures or feelings in other people's minds, too.

Here I am. I will write some of my thoughts in the thought bubble.

Who Has Thoughts?

I have thoughts. My parent has thoughts. Brothers and sisters have thoughts. Grandparents have thoughts. My teacher has thoughts. Children at school have thoughts. People I have never seen before have thoughts.

Everyone has thoughts.

Thoughts

Hopes Are Thoughts

Hopes are thoughts that make me feel good. Hopes are things that I want to happen. Sometimes they happen soon and sometimes they happen much later. Sometimes hopes don't ever happen. But thinking about them can still make me feel good. There might be things that I can do to help make my hopes happen.

I hope that _____

_____

_____

_____ .

No one knows my hopes unless I tell them or show them what my hopes are. I can tell my hopes to these *important people* in my life:

1. _____

2. _____

3. _____

4. _____

Thoughts

Fears Are Thoughts

Fears are thoughts that make me feel afraid or worried. Everyone has fears, sometimes.

Sometimes I feel afraid when I don't know what is going to happen. I might cry. I might yell. I might be very quiet.

When I have fears or when I am afraid, *I can to talk to someone who cares about me.* My parent and my teacher care about me. But they don't know my fear unless I tell them or unless I write it down and show them what I have written. Here are the names of some of the *important people who I can talk to* when I am afraid.

1 _____   3 _____

2 _____   4 _____

I can talk to one of these people and tell them my thoughts. I can tell them when I feel afraid. They will not make fun of me for being afraid. They will listen to me. **Sometimes I am afraid that** _____

_____

_____

_____ .

Thoughts

Imagination: About Pretend Things

Many children with autism only have thoughts about things that they can actually see and hear and touch.

But some children with high functioning autism or Aspergers have lots of **imagination.**

I will ⟨circle⟩ or highlight what is true for me. ✏

> ▶ I usually think about actual things that I can see and hear and touch in the **real world**. I do not like to pretend.
>
> ▶ I have lots of imagination.
>
> ▶ I like to pretend.

Having lots of imagination means that my mind might often be filled with thoughts about pretend things. Sometimes I might pretend so much that I forget that I am in the real world. The *real world* is my home and my school and the other places and people I know.

It can be fun for me to pretend. But it might not be very fun for other people to be near me when I am in my fantasy world. They might not like to pretend as much as I do. Other people are in the real world.

If having too much imagination is a problem at school or at home, then my **schedule** can show me when it is "imagination time". Sometimes it is time for pretending, and sometimes it is time for the real world.

Thoughts

Other People's Thoughts

Other people have pictures or words or feelings in their minds, too. They have their own thoughts. Their thoughts are quiet. *I cannot hear or see or feel other people's thoughts.* Only *they* know their thoughts.

**My thoughts are different
than other people's thoughts.**

Other people's thoughts are like a box that is closed. I cannot see what is inside a closed box. I do not know what thoughts are inside other people's minds unless they tell me.

Who Knows My Thoughts?

I know my own thoughts. I can see or hear or feel my thoughts. My thoughts are in my mind.

Other people cannot see or hear or feel my thoughts.

My mind is like a box with my thoughts inside. No one knows what is inside except me. Sometimes people can guess what I am thinking by looking at my face and my eyes, but they don't know for sure. My parent or teacher or another person cannot know my thoughts unless I tell them.

When I tell someone my thoughts, it is like opening the box so they can see what is inside.

Telling someone my thoughts, or **writing** my thoughts down and giving them to my parent or teacher or friends, is called **communicating.**

For Parents and Teachers

"How was school today? Did they have try-outs for the play?" said the therapist as he greeted the teenager with Asperger Syndrome. "YOU know!" said the teenager. "No, I don't know," replied the therapist. "You DON'T?" exclaimed the teenager, annoyed with disbelief.

Assumptions

Your child may assume that you know what she has experienced at school even though you were not there. She may assume that you know what she is thinking. She may assume that *you* are thinking the *same thing* that she is thinking.

Matters can be complicated further; one adult with autism explained that he isn't always sure if he has simply *thought* something or if he has actually *said it aloud*. When recalling memories of his childhood, he now realizes that he often assumed that he had spoken, and that others heard him, when in reality, he had only *thought* the words to himself.

Comic Strip Conversations

Comic Strip Conversations are interactive strategies that can be used to help us understand the child's assumptions about a social situation. Comic Strip Conversations use "thought bubbles" and other symbols to visually depict social interactions. With colored pens and paper, the adult and child draw stick figures to represent the child and others in the environment, and fill in bubbles to demonstrate what was said, what people's thoughts might have been, and the emotional content. This strategy helps the adult find out the child's perceptions and assumptions about people and other perplexing situations.

Carol Gray, in *Social Stories UnLimited: Teaching Social Skills with Social Stories and Comic Strip Conversations*, writes that Comic Strip Conversations "systematically identify what people say and do, and emphasize *what people may be thinking*.... Each Comic Strip Conversation regards the thoughts and feelings of others as holding equal *importance* to spoken words and actions in an interaction." She goes on to explain that "Comic Strip Conversations often provide insights into a student's perspective of a situation, and serve as an excellent prerequisite activity to the development of a social story." See the *Recommended Resources* at the end of this book for more information on Comic Strip Conversations.

Chapter 8: Communication

Workbook

Drawing by Thomas Johnson, 1995
Age 6

Communications

Communicating Is Natural to Most People

Most children in the world automatically *want to communicate.* They want to talk and share their thoughts and ideas with other people. They want to hear what other people think, and they like to listen to what other people are saying.

Communication is natural and easy for most children.

- That is why most children always seem to be in groups at recess. *They talk and laugh and yell.*

- They play together.

- They cluster around the same tables in the classroom.

- They talk all the time at lunch and want to sit next to each other whenever they can.

- They work quietly by themselves only when the teacher tells them that they *have to.*

Communication might feel *different* to me. Communication might not always be easy, natural, or fun, for children with autism.

Communications

Communicating
Is Not Always Natural to Me

Many children with autism might not automatically want to communicate when they see other people. They might not want to listen to what someone is saying. It might feel unnatural. They might not know what to say or they might not know when to stop talking. Doing *other things*, rather than communicating, might make children with autism happy. Some children enjoy being alone, or they might like to talk and play with someone who has the same interest.

I will (circle) or highlight what is true for me. ✏

- ▶ I usually do not like to listen when people are talking.
- ▶ I usually do not like to answer questions and talk to people.
- ▶ There is nothing I want to say.
- ▶ It's hard to figure out when to talk.
- ▶ I would rather do something else, instead of talking.
- ▶ I like to listen and talk to people. I like to communicate.
- ▶ Sometimes, talking with children can be stressful and confusing. It is not always very fun.
- ▶ Sometimes, it is fun for me to talk and play with children.
- ▶ Sometimes I get disappointed when I try to talk to others.
- ▶ I do not understand why children say _____

  _____ .

- ▶ It is more fun for me to _____ .

The Process of Communication

The process of communication is:

- putting my thoughts into **words**,

- getting someone's attention and **telling** them the words,

- **listening** to what that person says,

- **thinking** about what that person said,

- and then returning to the first step...**again**.

Communication moves in a circle, around and around between people.

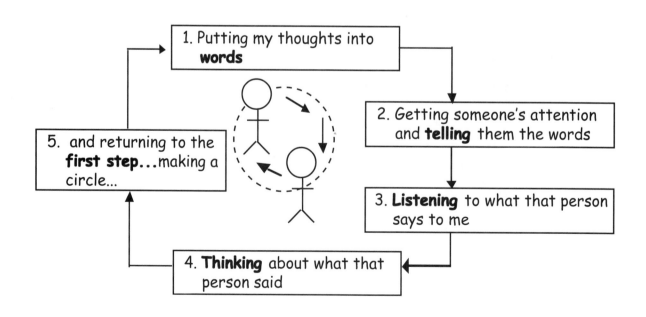

Putting My Thoughts Into Words

The most common way to communicate is by *talking*. I do this when I put my thoughts into words and then say the words to someone who is listening, in person or on the phone. Another common way to communicate is by *writing* or *typing.* After my thoughts are on paper, I can give the paper to someone, or send the paper to someone by mail. Another way to communicate is through *E-mail.*

I will (circle) or highlight what is true for me.

- ▶ I usually like to talk to people.
- ▶ I usually do not like to talk to people.
- ▶ I like to communicate by writing. Then I give it to the person.
- ▶ I like to communicate by typing. Then I print it and give it to the person.
- ▶ I like to communicate through E-mail.
- ▶ I would like to try typing or writing to communicate.
- ▶ I would like to try writing a letter.
- ▶ I do not like to talk or write.
- ▶ I would rather keep my thoughts to myself.
- ▶ I usually do not want to communicate.
- ▶ other: _____

Sentence Starters

These **sentence starters** might help put my thoughts into words. I can turn to this page when I want to say something, but don't have the words to begin. My parent or teacher can make me a copy of this page. I can use extra paper so there will be more room to write my thoughts in words. My parent or teacher can write other **sentence starters** for me, too.

I want to _____ .

Please help me with_____ .

The teacher said that _____ .

At school, I _____ .

What does " _____" mean?

Someone said that _____ .

I am thinking about _____ .

Is it true that _____ ?

I hope that _____ .

I am really happy that _____ .

I don't understand about _____ .

Making Sure Someone Is Listening

An important part of communication is getting someone's attention. In order for communication to happen, I must make sure that a person is ready to listen to me. I must make sure that he is paying attention.

Some children with autism might think that when they talk someone always listens, *but that is not always true.* The other person might not be listening if he is busy, or if he is thinking about something, or if he is talking with someone else.

> **When I talk, the other person might not hear what I am saying. For communication to happen, I need to make sure that the other person is ready to listen.**

How do I know if my parent or teacher or friend is paying attention and ready to listen to me?

- They are **ready to listen** if they have just asked me a question and they are looking at me.

- Usually if they are standing near me and if their eyes are looking toward me, they are **listening**.

- If they are **talking**, then they are **not ready to listen** to me.

Communications

*More about **making sure someone is listening**...*

- Sometimes my parent or teacher or friend is standing near me, but might **be doing something else, or listening to someone else**. Then I need to wait until the he or she is ready to listen to me.

- Before I talk, I can try to notice the direction her eyes are looking and see if she is **looking at another person who is talking**. If she is, it means that she is busy listening to someone else. She is not ready to listen to me, yet. I need to wait.

- If a person is talking on the telephone, or holding the phone quietly to her ear, it means that she is having a **phone conversation**. She is not ready to listen to me, yet. I need to wait.

- If I am not sure how long to wait, then I can softly tap the person on the shoulder one time, and say quietly:

> Excuse me, I have something to tell you.
> Please let me know when you are ready to listen.

- Then I try to **wait quietly** until the person tells me that he is ready to listen.

*More about **making sure someone is listening...***

Some children like to communicate by writing or typing.
I will (circle) or highlight what is true for me. ✎

I would like to:

▶ Write with a pen or pencil on paper. ✍

▶ Type on a keyboard and print it. 💻

▶ Type an E-mail on a computer. 💻

▶ Have a conversation by talking with people. 🗣

If I want to communicate in writing, I must remember to
give or send what I have written to a person. 🚶

I can either...

hand it to the person, or

put it in an envelope and mail it, or

send the E-mail.

Who Can I Communicate With?

There might be something that I want to say, but I might not know **who** to talk to.

These are the names of some of the children and adults with whom I can communicate:

1 _____   6 _____

2 _____   7 _____

3 _____   8 _____

4 _____   9 _____

5 _____   10 _____

There might be others, too. If there are others, I can write their names here, too:

_____

_____

_____

_____

_____

_____

Communications

Listening and Responding to What the Person Says

Communication is not just talking or writing. An important part of communication is **listening**. When the other person is talking, *I try to pay attention to what he or she is saying.*

While I am listening, I try to understand what is being said. If I do not understand, I can say:

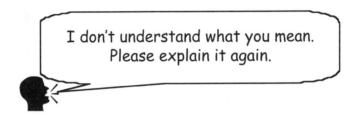

> I don't understand what you mean.
> Please explain it again.

For more help with understanding, see Chapter 6.

After I think about what the person said, then it is my turn to talk again. **Responding** is when I say something after I think about what the person said.

When my parent or teacher or friend and I listen and respond to each other, we are having a **conversation.**

I like to have conversations about _____

_____

_____ .

Communications

Why Conversations Can Be Confusing

Sometimes conversations can be confusing.

I will (circle) or highlight what is true for me. ✏

Conversations might be confusing because:

▶ I don't understand what the person is saying.

▶ Trying to make eye contact while I am talking and listening is difficult.

▶ I don't know when it's my turn to speak.

▶ I would rather think about something else.

▶ People are unpredictable; I am surprised at what they say.

▶ Too much sensory information (sights, sounds, touches...)

▶ I don't always agree with what is said; it makes me angry.

▶ Someone laughs, but it's not funny.

▶ Someone might make fun of me.

▶ I don't understand why should I talk.

▶ I don't have anything else to say.

▶ It's difficult to put my thoughts into words.

▶ The other person doesn't understand me.

▶ I am smarter than other people.

▶ I don't know who to talk to or who is talking to me.

▶ I don't know when to start or stop talking.

▶ The other person is not interested in what I am saying.

▶ I might say stupid things.

▶ other: _____

Communications

Talking Too Much

Some children talk a lot and some children talk a little.

Some children **talk too much**. They might talk so much that no one else can have a turn to talk. They might not listen to what other people say. They might not know when to stop talking.

It is difficult for most people to have a conversation with someone who talks too much. **Usually, it is not fun for people to be with someone who talks too much.**

If my parent or teacher says that I talk too much, we can try to understand why.

I will ⟨circle⟩ or highlight what is true for me. ✏

I might talk too much because:

- ▶ I don't know when I am supposed to stop talking.
- ▶ I like to talk about my special interest.
- ▶ I want to show how smart I am.
- ▶ I want people to like me.
- ▶ I am very excited or enthusiastic about what I am saying.
- ▶ I feel worried, upset, or anxious.
- ▶ I don't want the subject to change.
- ▶ I don't want the other person talk about something else.
- ▶ other: _____

Asking the Same Question

Most children ask questions. When the question is answered, they usually do not ask the same question again.

Some children with autism never ask questions, but some children with autism repeat the same question again and again. *If I repeat questions again and again, we can try to understand why.*

I will (circle) or highlight what is true for me. 🖉

I might ask the same question repeatedly because:

- ▶ I like to hear the answer.
- ▶ I want to hear if the answer is the same as before.
- ▶ I am worried or anxious.
- ▶ I like to watch people's faces while they give the answer.
- ▶ It's fun to ask the same question again.
- ▶ I don't remember the answer.
- ▶ I don't understand the answer.
- ▶ I want to ask something else, but I can't find the words.
- ▶ other: _____

One of the questions I like to ask is: _____

_____ ?

The usual answer is: _____

_____ .

Not Talking

Some children with autism do not talk very much at all. They might be very quiet at school or when they are with certain people. They might not want to talk about certain subjects. They are called *quiet children*.

Parents and teachers sometimes worry about quiet children and wonder why the children do not talk. They want the children to communicate more. They want to know what the children are thinking and feeling.

If my parent or teacher says that I don't talk enough or if there are times when I do not talk at all, we can try to understand why.

I will ⟨circle⟩ or highlight what is true for me. 🖉

I am quiet because:

▶ There is too much happening at the same time.

▶ I am feeling upset, worried, anxious, or angry.

▶ It is not the right place to talk.

▶ It is not with the right person to talk to.

▶ I don't know when to talk.

▶ There is no reason to talk.

▶ I might like to try writing or typing, instead of talking.

▶ other: _____

▶ other: _____

Communications

I will write in the blanks if I know what is true for me. 🖉

About talking with certain people:

I do not like to talk to _____ .

I like to talk to _____ .

I will talk to _____ .

I want to talk to _____ .

Other: _____ .

About certain subjects or ideas:

I want to talk about _____ .

I do not want to talk about _____ .

Other: _____ .

I do not talk because _____

_____

_____ .

Communications

Styles of Speaking

There are different **styles of speaking.**

People who grow up in different geographic areas might speak with a different accent or use a different dialect. Accents or dialects make words sound different.

People who are from a different country often speak English with a foreign accent. People in the United States speak English differently that people who live in England.

Sometimes children with autism have different styles of speaking. **I can ask someone to help me mark what is true for me. My style of speaking is:** 🖉

- ▶ Formal
- ▶ Soft or quiet
- ▶ Loud
- ▶ In a methodical rhythm
- ▶ High-pitched
- ▶ Monotone
- ▶ Fast
- ▶ Slow
- ▶ In a different accent than my family
- ▶ Other: _____

I am the only person who talks like me. That's OK!

Communications

Ending a Conversation

Some conversations between people are short; they might last less than a minute. Some conversations are long; long conversations might last an hour or more.

It is often difficult for people with autism to **know when a conversation should end.**

I might like to talk about something so much that I keep talking and talking. I might not notice if the other person has stopped listening or wants to do something else.

Sometimes, the *other person talks too much* and doesn't know that I do not understand what they are talking about. I do not know how to stop them.

Every conversation is different and every person is different. The same person might sometimes want a short conversation and other times want a long conversation.

- My teacher or my parent or someone else can help me practice *ending a conversation.*

- If I talk a lot, I might learn to ask **"Is it time to end this conversation?"**

- If I don't want to listen or talk at all, I can politely say **"I can't listen or talk right now, please."**

Communications

Talking to Myself

Most of the time people talk when they want to communicate with a person. Most people do not talk aloud to themselves. But some children **talk to themselves**. My parent or teacher will tell me if other people hear me talking to myself .

I will (circle) or highlight what is true for me. ✏

If I talk to myself, it might be because:

▶ I don't know that I am talking aloud.

▶ I am repeating something that I have heard.

▶ I am saying words or sounds that are pleasing to me.

▶ I am saying what I am thinking about.

▶ I am getting ready to talk to someone. I am practicing.

If children hear me talk to myself, they might laugh at me. That does not mean that I am bad or wrong. They laugh because most people do not talk to themselves, and they are not used to hearing it.

If I want to stop talking to myself, I can try to:

• Whisper.

• Think the words, instead of saying them aloud.

• Write my thoughts on paper or on the computer.

• Talk to myself in a private place where no one else can hear.

Communications

Asking for Help

It is natural for most children to ask for help. One of the first things babies learn is that when they *cry* someone will come and help them. Soon they learn to ask for help by *pointing,* and finally they ask for help by *talking.* Most children find it easy to ask for help when they need it.

It might be different for children with autism. Some children with autism *don't like* to ask for help. Some do not know *how* or *when* to ask for help. Many children with autism don't realize that they *can* get help or that *someone is there to help* them. Sometimes they might need help but don't want to ask because they think that it means they are *stupid.* Sometimes a child will get into the habit of asking for help *all the time,* even if he doesn't really need help.

Asking for help does not mean that I am stupid. All children ask for help sometimes. **It is good to ask for help when:**

- I don't understand what someone is saying.
- I don't understand what I am supposed to do.
- I know what I am supposed to do, but can't do it.
- I have tried my best to do something without help, but it just does not work out.

I can remember to say: **Can you help me, please?**

I can cut this sign out and tape it to my desk to remind me what to say.

Being Honest and Polite

Being honest means to say what is true. It is good to tell the truth. When my parent or teacher asks me a question, it is important to answer with the truth.

Sometimes though, I say something that is true, but it hurts a person's feelings. **Being polite** means not saying things that will hurt someone's feelings.

Some things that are not polite to say, are if a person:

- is fat, skinny, ugly, or unintelligent.

- has hair that looks funny, or no hair at all.

- is wearing clothes that look bad or wrong.

- other: _____

- other: _____

My parent or teacher or friend and I can make a list on the next page of the things that are not polite for me to say. I should probably not say these things aloud about a person, even if they are true.

I can be honest and tell the truth, but I can try *not to hurt someone's feelings*. I can be *polite*.

*More on **being honest and polite**...*

It is difficult to know which words will hurt someone's feelings. If I want to say something, but I am not sure if it is polite, I might start by saying:

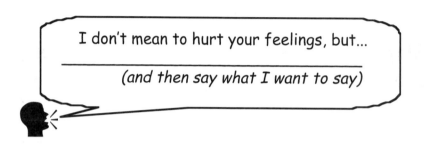

I don't mean to hurt your feelings, but...
_____
(and then say what I want to say)

If I often say things that aren't polite, my parent or teacher or friends can help me make a list of things that I can try to remember not to say. *I will try not to say:*

1. _____

2. _____

3. _____

4. _____

5. _____

If there are more, we can write them on a separate piece of paper.

Humor

When people have a **sense of humor** it means that they say and enjoy funny things. People with a *good sense of humor* can also laugh about themselves. There are different types of humor. I will ask my parent or teacher help me fill in the lines below.

- **Slapstick** is the kind of humor in cartoons and in some movies. *The Three Stooges* are famous for slapstick. Other slapstick that I have seen, is:_____.

- **Dry humor** is when people seem serious but they are *really* saying something funny. If I know someone who uses dry humor, his or her name is

  _____.

- **Puns** are jokes that use words that sound the same but mean different things. An example of a pun is _____ and _____.

- **Exaggeration** is when things are described differently on purpose to make them sound funny. An example of this was when:

  _____.

- **Sarcasm** is a type of humor that can be mean. It might hurt people's feelings. _____is someone we know who sometimes says sarcastic things.

Communications

- **Jokes** and **riddles** are memorized statements or questions that are funny to some people. If I have a favorite joke or riddle, it is:

_____

_____

_____

_____

Everyone might not laugh at my jokes.
Different people laugh at different things.

I will ⬭circle⬭ or highlight what is true for me. ✏

▶ Sometimes I try to say funny things or to tell jokes, but people don't laugh.

▶ Sometimes I make people laugh without even trying. I do not understand why they laugh. I didn't try to make a joke.

▶ Sometimes I laugh when I hear or say particular sounds, words, phrases, and questions.

▶ Some things that make me laugh are:

_____

_____

_____

Communications

Why People Laugh
When I'm Not Making a Joke

There are times when children say something that isn't a joke, but other children or adults will laugh.

I will (circle) or highlight what is true for me. ✏

- ▶ Sometimes people laugh when I say something, but I am not making a joke or trying to be funny.
- ▶ I do not like it when people laugh and it's not a joke.
- ▶ When people laugh, I get confused.
- ▶ I *do* like it when people laugh, even if I do not understand why. It makes me laugh too.

People might laugh when they hear something that they do not expect. They are surprised. It makes them laugh. Many children with autism think and talk *literally*. Some literal things are funny, like *puns*.

If people laugh, it doesn't mean that there is something wrong with me. It might mean that people enjoy being with me. If I am confused when people laugh, I can try to find out why they are laughing. I can say,

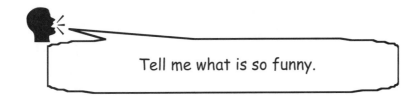

Tell me what is so funny.

Communications

Communicating With Art

Some people like to communicate with art. Examples of art are drawing, painting, singing, playing a musical instrument, dancing, drama, and writing poetry or stories. **I will mark what is true for me.** ✏

> ▶ I like to do art. I like to _____.
>
> ▶ I try to *communicate ideas* with my art. I want other people to understand my art.
>
> ▶ My art is not for communication. *I am not* trying to express my ideas to anyone else. I just like doing it.
>
> ▶ I do not like to do art.

If I try to communicate my ideas and thoughts with art, I have to remember that people who see or hear my art will think their own thoughts. When they hear or read or see or my art, their ideas might be different from what I want to say. They might not always understand exactly what I am trying to express.

If I want my parent, teacher, or friends to know something important, I need to do one of these things:

1. Put it into words and **tell** the person.
2. **Write** it down in words, and give it to the person.
3. **Type** it on a keyboard, print it, and give it to him.
4. Send the words by **mail** or **e-mail** to the person.

I can still enjoy doing my art, but I should also try to communicate in one of those four ways ————

For Parents and Teachers

When discussing an incident at work which resulted from a lack of communication with his co-worker, John Engle said that the co-worker was...

> *"....just some guy making noise. That's what people do. I don't really see why I was supposed to respond, or how I was supposed to respond. What was I supposed to say?*
>
> *I guess I don't go by the same rule book as most people."*

Ideas in This Chapter

✓ Language and communication are two different things

✓ Being verbal does not necessarily mean that a child is communicative

✓ Significant differences from an early age

✓ Speech and language evaluation

✓ Use this book

✓ Experiment with writing or typing

✓ Provide written cues

✓ Making conversation easier

Language and communication are two different things

Communication is more than the development of verbal skills. Many children with autism develop verbal language skills separately from learning to communicate. From the very beginning, learning to say words is not automatically linked with communication. An often-cited example is the child with autism who repeats commercials or recites the complete dialogue from animated videos, but rarely uses these highly developed verbal skills for communicative intent.

In young children who don't have autism, the acquisition of language and communication is one and the same. For them, words automatically and powerfully function as tools for communication.

Being verbal does not necessarily mean that a child is communicative

Most children with high functioning autism, even those with highly developed verbal skills, have significant glitches in their awareness and understanding about essential aspects of communication and conversation. Social communication skills usually lag behind verbal development even in these very verbal children. Ordinary communicative functions may be impaired, such as: the ability to get someone's attention; initiate communication; conversational skills, such as responding and building on what is being said; and the ability to sustain a reciprocal interaction.

Significant differences from an early age

Discreet skills and behaviors which form the backbone of communication generally emerge for most typically developing children between infancy and the toddler years. It is said that an infant's eyes first focus at the distance of approximately ten inches, the distance from his eyes to mother's eyes when

cradled in her arms, illustrating the early bonding that connects one to another. During the first two years of life, most children become proficient at following another's line of gaze, and using eye contact and gestures to meet their needs and for communication and social interaction.

These powerful communicative behaviors happen easily and naturally. They do not have to be intentionally taught to most babies. Whatever it is in the brain that ignites awareness of being connected to others, perceives multiple perspectives, and drives social communicative skills, is already present in typically developing infants at birth. Communication skills are the culmination of an elaborate cluster of versatile behaviors and perceptions that merge to create meaningful engagement. The ease with which this takes place is a result of the way the *neurotypical—non-autistic—* brain functions.

The distinct communicative styles found in children with autism, too, result from the way the brain functions from infancy. Autism results in particular patterns of thinking, attention, and learning styles. Maybe these babies' perceptions are flooded with sensory experiences that are so entertaining, distracting, overwhelming, or even disturbing, that these experiences take precedence over the need to communicate. Maybe they are paying attention to isolated and unconnected details, and do not see the relationships between them. Maybe they become so engrossed in one thing that they are not able to notice other factors in the environment. Most toddlers with autism demonstrate that they don't fully understand that there is a powerful connection between their needs and purposeful spontaneous action resulting in desired changes. Simple accomplishments like getting someone's attention and directing their attention to something–even the simple act of initiating communication–appear to be foreign concepts.

By parent report, we learn that some babies, later diagnosed with autism, were extremely passive. Others were very demanding and cried but could not be comforted. Their mother's attempts to ease their cries didn't seem to soothe. Who can begin to imagine what the baby with autism experiences as it tries to make sense of the world around him? *No wonder adults with autism often point out that the world runs on rules which weren't made for them.*

Speech and language evaluation

A speech and language therapist should look carefully at your child's pragmatic use of language and his everyday functional and social communication skills. Which specific areas need teaching and practice?

Use this book

Reread the appropriate pages in this chapter with your child when he encounters awkward or troubling experiences due to communication difficulties. You might add a time on his schedule for rereading particular pages. With the open book, identify and review the basic elements of communication and conversation, while relating them to the real issue that has occurred.

Experiment with writing or typing

Have a keyboard, or pen and paper, available for frequent use. During relaxed times, free time, or recreational time, experiment by communicating in writing. Do it frequently enough so it becomes familiar. Help him become used to writing or typing, in a variety of situations, for a variety of reasons, just for fun. *By practicing on a regular basis, you will lay the groundwork for using written communication at difficult moments when there is a need for communication.* When he resists or is unable to communicate verbally during times of stress, or if his attempts at communicating are ineffective, the tools of written communication will already be familiar to him and to you, his partner in communication.

There are times that your child needs to (or is expected to) communicate, but he is unable to do so in an appropriate manner. Offer him the now familiar keyboard or pen and paper. *Free from the complexities of face-to-face talking*, he may

discover this to be a clearer route to communication. You might write sentence starters for him, as demonstrated earlier in this chapter. *Allow his attention to be on the written or typed word, and not on you.* Eye contact is not important while using this strategy.

Provide written cues

In situations when your child isn't spontaneously communicating, doesn't get someone's attention, won't ask for help or for something that he needs or wants, you can provide visual cues to make it easier. For example, let's say that your child doesn't ask for help when he needs it. He might sit passively and not do anything at all. He might get stuck in one activity because he can't go on. He might become very frustrated, anxious, or upset. The following ideas are examples of written cues that can help him initiate communication. Notice how the level of structure and specificity is slightly different in each of the four ideas. Your child might need more or less structure depending on the situation and how he feels on a particular day. You can try one or more of the following:

 Write a rule.

Be concise, specific, and concrete. Post it where it can be seen.

> When I don't understand what to do,
> I raise my hand and ask for help.

 Write a list of phrases to fit the situation.

Have him review it frequently, especially prior to the situation. If necessary, post it in the situation where it is needed.

> I can ask my teacher for help, when I need it. I can say:
> "Can you help me please?" or
> "Please help me," or
> "I don't understand what to do now."

 Write a "cue card" with the exact wording for a specific situation.

Place this written cue in the appropriate location. When you notice that he needs help, draw his attention to the cue card so he will read it. Have the appropriate person respond to his request. For example, a card containing this wording is posted in the inside of his locker.

> "Will you please help me with the zipper of my coat?"

✍ **Supplement the visual cue with a social story to clarify the situation.**

Describe the situation in a straightforward manner, from the perspective of the child. Describe the perspective of others where relevant. The social story will give the child a way to more accurately interpret what is happening, and help make sense of what he is supposed to do. Have him read the story ahead of time and keep it available for re-reading.

Asking For Help With My Blue Winter Coat

Our class goes outside for recess almost every day. On days that it is very, very cold, I wear my blue winter coat. I try to zip up my coat and sometimes I can do it myself. But other times the zipper on my blue winter coat gets stuck. When it gets stuck, I try and try, but the zipper just doesn't move.

While the kids get ready for recess, they sometimes say "Hurry up". They tell me to hurry up because they are happy that it is recess. They cannot go outside until everyone, including me, is standing in line. But I do not want to stand in line until my coat is zipped up. Sometimes I get worried and start to cry. Sometimes I get angry when they say "Hurry up".

When the zipper is stuck, I can try to remember to ask for help. I can walk to my teacher or the assistant and say "Will you please help me? My zipper is stuck." Then my coat will be zipped up and I can stand in line. Then the whole class, including me, can go outside for recess.

Making conversation easier

Explore ways that a conversation can be depicted visually, so he can *see* the reciprocity, the "back-and-forth essence" of the interaction, the connection and the relationships between the statements, *in a concrete way*. Try strategies that add structure and order to the potentially confusing, distracting, or annoying qualities of conversation, such as:

Using a computer

Have a conversation at the computer, sitting side by side. Take turns typing and talking simultaneously. Watch the dialogue appear on the screen as it is spoken.

E-mail

Much like colleagues in the same office who keep up a dialogue via E-mail, your child might build and sustain communication with you or friends more readily in this manner.

Topic Hat

Make a game of staying on the topic. Take turns drawing from a "topic hat." Topics can be placed into the hat which include plenty of personal favorites along with a variety of other subjects. Make up rules that would be most appropriate based on your child's unique needs. One of the rules might be to stay on each topic for a certain time limit. A variation of this rule might be for each person to make a certain number of statements and/or questions about the topic before the next one is chosen.

Comic Strip Conversations

As introduced on page 129, this strategy combines a visual representation of conversation along with the speakers' unspoken thoughts. Variations of this strategy can be tried to meet an individual's needs. Carol Gray has described Comic Strip Conversations as "the art of conversation." See the *Recommended Resources* at the end of this book for more information about Comic Strip Conversations.

Chapter 9: School

Workbook

Drawing by Maria White, 1999
Age 21

School

Different Kinds of Schools

Most big towns and cities have many different schools. *Preschools* are for very young children. Children in kindergarten or first grade begin *elementary school*. *Middle school* usually begins in the sixth grade. Sometimes there are *junior high schools* instead of middle schools. Students begin *high school* in the ninth or tenth grade.

There are *public schools* and *private schools*. There are *charter schools* and *parochial schools*. Some children do not go to a school at all. They are *home-schooled*. Some children do a *combination* of home-school and attending school.

I will ⟨circle⟩ or highlight what is true for me. ✏

- ▶ I go to a public school. I am in the _____ grade.
- ▶ I go to a charter school. I am in the _____ grade.
- ▶ I go to a private school. I am in the _____ grade.
- ▶ I go to a parochial school. I am in the _____ grade.
- ▶ I am home-schooled. My _____ is my teacher.
- ▶ other: _____

The ideas in this chapter might help me learn, and feel good about learning, no matter what kind of school I go to.

Knowing What Will Happen Today

Most children like to know what is going to happen in school. After I get used to a new teacher, I usually remember what will happen in that class. But things can *change*.

I will (circle) or highlight what is true for me. 🖉

▶ Often teachers announce what is going to happen, but I **don't always understand** exactly what they mean.

▶ Sometimes **I think** something is going to happen, but it **doesn't.**

▶ Sometimes things **change** and I don't understand why.

▶ The children and the teachers all seem to know what is going to happen, yet sometimes I get **confused**.

▶ I wonder when it will be time for my **favorite** things.

▶ I usually **ask** my teacher when certain things are going to happen. I wonder when _____ will happen?

▶ I often **tell** the teacher when something is supposed to happen. I get worried or angry if it doesn't happen on time.

▶ I like to be able to know when things will happen.

If I have a schedule, I can see *what* is going to happen, and *when* it is going to happen. I can use it every day.

For Parents and Teachers: Detailed information about using a schedule can be found on pp. 36-49.

A Place to Work

Everyone has a **place to work**.

Some teachers let the children choose where they want to sit. Sometimes children sit anywhere they want to, around a large table, with other children. Sometimes they sit at different places every day.

Sometimes, children have their own desks. The desks might be touching other desks, in *groups* or *pods*.

In other classrooms, the desks are lined up in rows, and they are not touching each other.

Some children might always work at their own desk. Some children might go to a different desk or table to work, sometimes.

Some children might go to a special place to work. It might be a regular desk, or it might be a desk with walls, or a study carrel. Sometimes this special desk is called an **office**.

The teacher decides how the desks will be arranged in the room. Sometimes the teacher might move the desks.

In the *classroom*, I work at _____

_____ .

At *home*, I do my work at _____

_____ .

My Own Office

An **office** is a special place for working. The school principal works in an office. Many adults work in offices. Maybe my parent works in an office. Offices are just for working. Offices help people work better.

I might have a special type of office at school. My office is made by putting up three short walls on my desk. The office walls help me pay attention to my work instead of other things in the room.

This is what my office might look like.

*More on **my own office**...*

My teacher can find the best place for my office. I might try working in different places until we find the right place for my office. My office might be:

- *At my desk.* I can put the office walls up when I work, and take them down when I am finished.

- *At a different desk in the classroom;* a desk used just for my office.

- *At a desk outside of my classroom* where it is quiet.

- *At a desk in a different classroom.*

Other children in my class might use offices, too. Offices help children focus on their work.

In my class, I have a _____

_____ .

My schedule shows me when it is time to work in my office. I might work in my office many times, every day.

Why It Might Be Hard to Work Independently

To **work independently** means that children work by themselves, without someone telling them what to do. *Children have to remember which assignments to do, when to start, how to do it, where it goes when it's finished, and what to do next.* Working independently can be difficult for many children with autism.

I will (circle) or highlight what is true for me. ✏️

It might be hard to work all by myself, because:

▶ There are too many things to remember.

▶ I don't know how to get started working.

▶ I don't know what to do first and what to do next.

▶ I don't understand how to do the work by myself.

▶ There is too much noise in the room or in the hall.

▶ I am busy watching and listening to children in the room.

▶ I am worried that the work might take too long.

▶ I'll just wait until someone comes to help me.

▶ There is too much to do.

▶ I am thinking about _____ .

▶ I wonder what is going to happen later.

▶ I would rather do something else.

▶ Other: _____ .

Being Independent and Organized With the Work System

When I do my work, I can follow a **work system**. The work system is a list of things to do. I don't need my teacher or assistant to *tell* me what to do, because the work system *shows* me what to do.

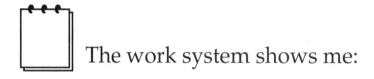 The work system shows me:

1. How many assignments am I supposed to do?
2. Which assignments am I supposed to do?
3. The progress I am making and when I am finished.
4. What will happen next?

My teacher or assistant will *teach me* how to follow the work system.

The work system helps me be more **organized**. I follow the work system by crossing out or checking off each assignment, **one at a time**. I can see exactly **how many assignments** I have left to do, the progress that I am making, and I can see what will happen **next**, after I am **finished**.

☑ I don't need my teacher or assistant to help me all the time. I can work independently when I follow my work system. *The work system makes it easy.*

Written Directions

Sometimes my teacher says that I must do an assignment or a job *by myself.* Sometimes I try to remember what to do, but sometimes I just wait for someone else to tell me what to do. **When I work, I might:** ✏

- ▶ Forget the directions.
- ▶ Get mixed up.
- ▶ Start thinking about something else.
- ▶ Have trouble staying focused.

There is a way for me to learn to do my assignments and jobs by myself. My teacher or assistant can teach me how to follow **written directions**.

I can find the *written directions* with each assignment or with the materials for each job. The directions are written clearly and literally, in the order that I will follow. I read the first line and then do it.

I check it off or cross it out. Then I read the next one and do what it says. Then I check it off or cross it out. *I follow each step until I am finished.* Then my job or assignment is done.

School

Knowing What Is Most Important

Most children know what **important** means. They can read something or listen to a story and know what is important in that story. Sometimes important things in one story are not important in a another story. Most children can figure this out.

My teacher or parent might tell me that I need to find what is *most important* in a story, or tell me *to pay attention* to something in the written directions.

- Children with autism are good at seeing or noticing lots of *details*, especially details that are very interesting to them.

- Many of the details that I notice, may not be considered important by my teacher.

- It helps if someone can show me which details are *most important*. My teacher or assistant can:

underline

circle

star ★

check ✓

or

... the most important details in an assignment, on a story, on my schedule, and on my written directions.

Handwriting

Some children with autism like to print or write. It is easy for them. They like the way it looks and their handwriting is easy for other people to read.

But there are many children with high functioning autism or Asperger Syndrome who find it very difficult to write. They might know what they want to write, but when they try to use a pencil or a pen, *it doesn't look right.*

When that happens, some children might not want to do their school work or homework. It might be too difficult or frustrating.

It is important for children to practice writing or printing. Therapists can give teachers and parents ideas that can help.

But children should also be able to do their work and put their ideas on paper, without always being frustrated.

If writing frustrates me, I might be able to learn to do my work with a keyboard on a word processor, or on a computer. **I will mark what is true for me.** ✐

  ▶ I like my work to look good.

  ▶ I would like to learn to use a **keyboard** or a **computer** for my school work or homework.

  ▶ I do **not** want to do my assignments on a computer. I want to write my work with a pen or pencil.

  ▶ other: _____ .

Using My Special Interests

There are a lot of things to learn in school. But sometimes a lesson just doesn't make sense, or I don't know what it means. I can't concentrate on it.

But my *special interests* mean a lot to me. I can understand and remember what I read about my special interests.

I might be able to learn new things if my teacher uses my special interests to teach me. **It is usually easier for me to learn when it involves my special interests.**

The subjects or classes that *don't make sense* to me are:

1. _____

2. _____

3. _____

My special interests are:

1. _____

2. _____

3. _____

There is more about my special interests on pages 22-23.

The Computer

Most children like to use computers. Many children with autism are very skilled on the computer.

I like using the computer. (Circle what is true:) **YES** or **NO**

Sometimes it is easier to learn something new on the computer, than to learn it from a person.

Computers can be used for many things: work, free time, communication, or having fun with a friend.

I might be very good on the computer. I might want to use the computer all the time. My *schedule* will show me when it is time for the computer and when it is time to do other things.

- Sometimes my schedule will show *free time* on the computer. Then I can make a choice of what I want to do on the computer.

- Sometimes my schedule will show *work time* on the computer. This means that I have an assignment on the computer. I can follow the directions at the computer.

School

School Jobs

The principal has a job. The cafeteria workers have jobs. The custodians have jobs. The teachers have jobs. Students have the job of doing their work and learning.

Some children can have other jobs too. **School jobs** for children can be:

- sorting mail in the office
- delivering messages
- taking reports to the office
- collecting attendance sheets
- shelving or straightening library books
- dusting shelves
- taking lunchroom chairs down/putting them up
- watering plants
- cleaning mirrors
- sorting and recycling
- other:

A job that sounds interesting to me is _____ .

Maybe I can have a job in school. First, someone can teach me how to do the job. Then if I still need help, I can follow the *written directions*.

Free Time

Sometimes the teacher says that it is **free time**. Free time can be different with every teacher.

Some teachers say that free time must be *quiet*. Other teachers say that children can *talk* with each other during free time. Some teachers say that children must stay at their *desks* during free time. Other teachers say that children can *walk* around the room during free time. Some teachers say that children can walk or sit only in *certain areas* of the room during free time. Other teachers might say that it is free time after work is *finished*. Another teacher might say that it is free time at *the end of the day.*

Free time usually means that children can make choices. But even though it is called *"free"*, certain things are allowed, while other things are not. **Each teacher makes his or her own rules for free time.**

Free time can be difficult for many children with autism. **I will** ⬭circle⬮ **or** highlight **what is true for me.** ✏

> ▶ I am not sure what I am supposed to do at free time.

> ▶ Sometimes it is confusing or too noisy.

> ▶ Sometimes I get in trouble during free time.

> ▶ I would like to know **what I can do** during free time. If I see the choices, I can pick one.

> ▶ I would like to do something involving my special interest.

> ▶ other: _____ .

School

Knowing More About Free Time

I would like to know more about free time.

There is free time in my classroom, in the after-school program, in Boy Scouts or Girl Scouts, in clubs, at Sunday School, or at _____ .

I can make a copy of this page and take it to the teachers or the leaders. I can ask them to write down specific information about free time.

Rules and Choices for Free Time at _____

1. _____

2. _____

3. _____

4. _____

5. _____

6. _____

Rules

Rules are everywhere. There are rules in stores and in restaurants, on the street and in the neighborhood, at home and at school. There are rules about what to say, how and when to talk, how to behave, what to do, when to do it, and on and on.

Sometimes rules are written on signs so people can read them, but most rules are not written. These are called *unwritten rules*. Most children learn the unwritten rules just by watching and listening to others. Most children learn and follow *unwritten rules* without even thinking about it.

- Many children with autism have difficulty knowing and understanding *unwritten* rules.

- It might be easier for me to learn rules if they are **written** on a sign or piece of paper.

- When I can **read** the rules, I know exactly what they are.

- When rules are **literal, concrete, and specific**, I might understand them better.

School

*More on **rules**...*

Most children follow the rules because the rules make sense to them. When children understand the reasons for the rules, they can follow them more easily.

I might forget to follow a rule because *it might not make sense to me.*

I might need **more information** about some rules. Rules at school or at home that *I do not understand*, are:

1. _____

2. _____

3. _____

4. _____

5. _____

6. _____

If there are more, I can write them on a separate piece of paper.

Reading a **social story** might help me understand. My parent or teacher can write a social story. When I understand more about the situation surrounding the rule, I might be able to remember and follow it more often.

Then, when I read the rule, it will make sense to me.

Homework

Children have four different types of work for school. The first two types of work happen when *I am in school.*

1. Independent work in school - This is work that I do at my desk or in my office at school. I do independent work by myself, using a work system or written directions.

2. Work in school with another person - This is work that I do in school with my teacher, assistant, tutor, or another child.

Other work is done *at home.* There are two kinds of homework:

3. Independent homework - This is the work I do by myself at home. I can follow a work system and written directions at home, too.

4. Homework with another person - This is the work that I do with help, at home.

When I get home from school, I check my after-school schedule. I can see when it is time to do homework and when it is time for other things.

School

Good Grades

Children earn grades for their work at school. Some grades are letters and some grades are numbers.

Everyone likes to get good grades. The highest grades are usually A+ or 100, but there are *other good grades, too.*

For example, good letter grades might be C, C+, B-, B, B+, A-, A, and A+.

I will (circle) or highlight what is true for me. ✎

- ▶ I like to get good grades.
- ▶ Good grades make me feel happy and proud.
- ▶ I have to get the highest grade.
- ▶ I do not like to make mistakes.
- ▶ I get angry or upset if I do not get the highest grade.
- ▶ It is OK if I make some mistakes.
- ▶ I want to know which grades are good grades.
- ▶ If I get good grades, then I am happy.
- ▶ I do not care about grades.
- ▶ other: _____

Different teachers use different grades.

If I am concerned about getting good grades, I can ask my teachers to write down the numbers or letters or symbols that are considered good grades in their classes.

I can make a copy of the next page for my teachers.

*More on **good grades**...*

Different teachers use different grading scales. Grades can be letters, numbers, checks, or other symbols. I am concerned about getting good grades. I will find out what are considered good grades in all of my classes.

(My parent or teacher and I can make a copy of this page. I will take it to my teachers for them to fill in.)

Teacher's Name:

The good grades in this class are:

Teacher's Name:

The good grades in this class are:

Teacher's Name:

The good grades in this class are:

Teacher's Name:

The good grades in this class are:

The Quiet Area

There are a lot of sounds and noises and people in school. There are a lot of things to remember. There are a lot of things that I am supposed to do. *Being in school takes a lot of concentration for children with autism.*

Sometimes I feel **overwhelmed**. *Overwhelmed* means that I feel confused; there is too much going on at the same time.

I will ⟨circle⟩ or highlight what is true for me. ✏

Sometimes in school:

> ▶ I feel worried or anxious.
>
> ▶ I might refuse to do my work.
>
> ▶ I might cry or yell.
>
> ▶ I might get very quiet.
>
> ▶ I feel overwhelmed.
>
> ▶ I wish that I could be by myself where it is quiet.

I might have a **quiet area** in school. The quiet area is a good place. I can take a break from all the busy things that happen in school when I go to the quiet area. The quiet area helps me stay calm. After being in the quiet area, I go back to work or to the classroom activity.

My schedule can show me when it is time for the quiet area. I can learn to tell my teacher when I need to go to the quiet area.

Teaching Other Children About Autism

This book is helping me learn about autism and how it affects me.

Other children need to learn about autism, too, so they can understand how autism affects all of us, together.

When other children know about autism, they might understand me better. They will learn that I am OK the way I am. They will learn that autism is another way of being.

I will (circle) or highlight what is true for me. 🖉

- ▶ I want my friends to understand about autism.
- ▶ I want children in my class to understand about autism.
- ▶ I want _____ (name) to know about autism.
- ▶ I would like to show this book to_____ .
- ▶ I want my friends to see this book.
- ▶ I don't want my friends to see this book.
- ▶ I especially want my friends to see *certain pages* of this book. I will show my parent which pages are *important*.
- ▶ Other: _____ .

School

My Thoughts About School

1. My favorite thing about school is _____ .

2. In school, I also like _____ .

3. In school, I do not like _____ .

4. _____ is the hardest thing for me at school.

5. _____ is the easiest thing for me at school.

6. The things that help me the most at school, are

_____ .

7. It bothers me when _____ .

8. I wish that _____ .

9. I would like to learn more about _____ .

10. I do not understand about _____ .

11. I would like to be friends with _____ .

For Parents and Teachers

"My pace is not school's pace."

–Maria White at age 16

Ideas in This Chapter

✓ The educational environment

✓ Remember the schedule!

✓ Problems when teaching independent work skills

✓ The one-to-one assistant

✓ Making an office

✓ How can I use a work system to teach my child to work independently?

✓ Providing written directions

✓ Written directions can be used at home, too

✓ Organizing the work space, supplies, and materials

✓ Modifying worksheets

✓ Folder tasks

✓ Student satisfaction and motivation

✓ Utilizing special interests

✓ Outlines, diagrams, models, notes, and mapping

✓ Nine types of lesson adaptations

✓ Group instruction

✓ The computer: *A cautionary measure*

✓ Homework

✓ What are the *most important* skills I should teach?

✓ More educational interventions

✓ The quiet area

✓ Why is he like that?

✓ Programs to teach peers about differences

✓ Talking about autism and your child

The educational environment

Which classroom is best for my child? Where will he learn best? Where will he be the happiest? calmest? most motivated? most challenged? Should the school system hire a special assistant for him? Should he be home-schooled? Should he go to a private school? What about full inclusion? What about a special education class? What is the best educational environment for children with high functioning autism?

 Parents and teachers can agonize over these questions, and rightly so. Your child may not fit perfectly in any of the options available in your community. There is no single right answer for all children with high functioning autism or Aspergers. Both informal and formal assessment is necessary. Take a close look at your child's skills, strengths, interests, needs, and the way he learns. What level of structure is optimum for him to function successfully, independently, and happily? What qualities in the environment help him thrive? What has worked in the past? What hasn't worked? Do any ideas in this book help? According to the TEACCH program*,

"....the basic aims of structured teaching remain relevant when teaching children with high-functioning autism and Asperger syndrome. First, structured teaching seeks to make the world, in this case, the classroom environment, as meaningful as possible. When the child genuinely understands what is happening and what is expected, learning is enhanced, and behavior problems decrease. Second, teaching children with autism involves a two prong approach that focuses on helping the child develop skills and competencies while also recognizing the need for environmental modifications to maximize student strengths and minimize student deficits.

These organizing principles underlie the primary strategies for structuring the classroom environment for students with high functioning autism and Asperger syndrome. The strategies include: (1) understanding autism, (2) understanding the unique child through both formal and informal assessment, (3) making events consistent and predictable, (4) clarifying instructions and expectations, (5) structuring tasks and assignments to promote success, and (6) cultivating and fully utilizing students' compelling interests."

---

*Linda Kunce and Gary B. Mesibov. (1998). "Educational Approaches to High-Functioning Autism and Asperger Syndrome", in *High Functioning Autism or Asperger Syndrome?* Plenum Press, New York, 1998, page 230. See the Recommended Resources at the end of this book.

While determining the best educational program for your child, review the previous workbook pages in this chapter and make a list of the strategies that were introduced. Some of the strategies are discussed in greater detail here.

Remember the schedule!

The schedule has been introduced in Chapter 2, and recommended again in subsequent chapters. It is no coincidence that it is, again, at the top of the list of suggestions. The schedule, usually in the form of a checklist for most high functioning children, serves as one of the major organizing strategies for your child.

Your child's schedule should be designed in a way that makes sense to him. You might have to try different adaptations until you see what is most effective. *Examples of several different types of schedules, as well as tips for using a schedule, can be found in Chapter 2, pages 36-49.*

Your child's ability to use the schedule independently will have far-reaching results, especially after completion of school. In North Carolina, we have found that the adults with autism who are able to use a schedule and follow a work system independently, are those who have greater success at keeping a job. *(See pages 167, 171-173, 178, 192, 194-196, and 209-210.)*

Problems when teaching independent work skills

It is not unusual for parents and children to sit hour upon hour every night, fighting a never-ending battle to keep up with class assignments. You may find yourself constantly helping, prompting, encouraging, directing, bribing, pampering, bargaining, or actually doing his homework. Needless to say, this is extremely frustrating for both child and adult.

Many children with autism have difficulty with one or more aspects of working independently.

For some children, the idea of doing work for *school* at *home* (homework) was so absurd that they flatly refuse to do it. A high-school student completed every assignment, but didn't understand that it was important to turn them in. It was only at the end of the semester after he had failed the class, that the school counselor discovered all the assignments, neatly stacked in his locker.

In order to develop independent work skills, the child must already know how to do the work. In some classrooms, it is not unusual to find that the assignments require skills that the child has not yet mastered. If this is the case, you cannot expect the child to practice working independently, *if he can't do the assignments by himself, anyway!* The level or amount of work might be inappropriate based on your child's abilities. In some cases, the assignments will need to be modified. Ways to organize, clarify, and modify assignments will be discussed later in this chapter. In other cases, his educational program may need to be reevaluated based on a current and accurate assessment of his skills and abilities.

More than likely, your child has developed the habit of waiting for help even if he *knows what to do!* The routine varies from child to child. Needing a prompt to begin, needing constant prompts to continue, needing someone to sit next to him, or needing someone to tell him when he is done and what to do next, become well-established routines. No amount of explaining why he must work independently seems to make a difference. Waiting him out only seems to delay and lengthen the inevitable. He simply can't or won't work independently.

If this is true for your child, then *learning to work independently* should be a primary educational focus and take top priority in his yearly educational goals. From TEACCH's long-range perspective of supporting children with autism as they grow into adults entering the job market, *the ability to work independently is more crucial than acquiring specific academic skills.*

The one-to-one assistant

One solution that school systems frequently employ when educating children with high functioning autism is to provide a personal assistant or a "one-to-one" assistant. The well-meaning assistant does what is necessary to get your child to pay attention, to participate in the classroom, and to complete his work. And although the goal is to "fade" this level of personal support, independence can be elusive.

Whether your child has a personal assistant, or whether he requires a great deal of attention from the teacher or help from other students, it is recommended that his helpers be clear on what the goal is and how to reach it. They must understand that their goal is *to teach him to use the structure which will allow him, in turn, to practice and develop independent work skills.* Your child must learn how to make sense of the environment and how to organize his behavior without someone prompting him. He must know how to find relevant information in the situation, and use this information to function independently.

On the previous workbook pages, your child has been introduced to the office *(p.169)*, the schedule *(pp. 31-32, 167)*, the work system *(p. 172)*, and written directions *(p. 173)*. These are essential tools to achieving and sustaining independent work skills during the school years and beyond.

Making an office

The *office* provides the physical structure to help your child focus on the work in front of him. When the office is "put up," or when your child sits at a special desk designated as his office, he is reminded that it is independent work time. Extra sights and sounds are eliminated.

An office should be portable yet sturdy. A good, inexpensive office can be made easily from a science fair display board, purchased at office supply stores. Cut the folding board in half, horizontally, creating two tri-folding cardboard screens. (Each display board makes two offices.) This inexpensive, sturdy office is preferable, in most cases, to buying new furniture or study carrels. It is portable, allowing for individualized use, and can be folded and stored when not needed.

You may want to keep a stack of offices available in your classroom for other students to pick up and use when they need to concentrate, too.

The work system has been taped to the inside wall of the "office."

How can I use a work system to teach my child to work independently?

The work system is a logical way to organize a series of assignments. For children who have good reading abilities, the work system is usually provided in the form of a written checklist. It provides four important pieces of information:

1. What work am I supposed to do?
2. How much work is there to do?
3. How do I stay on track and know when I am finished?
4. What will happen after all my work is finished?

A work system is used when he must complete a series of assignments or tasks.

<u>11:00 Independent Work in Office</u>

☑ 1. Reading - "Recipe Questions"
☐ 2. Geography - "Bordering States"
☐ 3. Spelling - Chap 16 words (5 times)
☐ 4. Fold Up office + Choose activity in <u>Activity Center</u>

After checking his schedule and seeing that it is time for *independent work,* your child goes to his designated office, or puts the cardboard office on his desk. He locates the work system, which has been written on a piece of paper, a clipboard, or a notepad. It may have been placed in or on his desk, or perhaps it is taped to the inside of his office *(see diagram p. 193)*. The work system will show him what he is to accomplish during this period of time.

It is important to note that the work system differs from what we typically think of as an "assignment list" in that it *always contains the four essential pieces of information* listed above. The tasks or assignments are listed in order. Your child checks them off or crosses them out as they are completed. The last entry on the list shows what to do next, after completing all the assignments. This final piece, *"what will happen after the work is finished"*, is an integral part of the work system, not normally found on assignment lists. By doing this, you have reinforced the concept of *"finished"* and you have structured the next transition. This provides your child with a sense of order and clarity about what will happen next.

Providing written directions

Written directions show the steps to follow when completing a single task or assignment. Each task is broken down into smaller steps, *based on your child's organizational needs and how much detail he requires.* The steps are listed in sequence and your child is taught to check off or cross out each step as he proceeds. Based on his responses, you might need to highlight certain words or pieces of information.

Below, are two sets of directions for completing the *same* assignment, but written for two different children. Both students require a high level of *structure* in order to work independently. Both sets of directions provide a clear sequence to follow, however *the directions have been individualized for each student.* The difference is that the directions on the *right* are even more specific and concrete, and provide more details than the directions on the left.

DIRECTIONS FOR
"Recipe Questions"

___ 1. Get "Recipe Questions" sheet for garlic bread.

___ 2. Get cookbook.

___ 3. Answer circled questions on sheet.

___ 4. Return cookbook to shelf.

___ 5. Put sheet in "finished work."

___ 6. Check work system.

Follow Directions for
"Recipe Questions"

☐ 1. Get what is needed:
  ☐ cookbook
  ☐ pen
  ☐ "Garlic Bread" sheet

☐ 2. Write name on sheet.

☐ 3. Open book - page 56

☐ 4. Read question #1

☐ 5. Write answer on sheet.

☐ 6. Read question #4

☐ 7. Write answer on sheet.

☐ 8. Read question # 5

☐ 9. Write answer on sheet.

☐ 10. Fold sheet + put in book.

☐ 11. Put book in "finished" tray.

☐ 12. Check to see what to do next (on work system).

Written directions can be used at home, too

Visual strategies can be used at home. Schedules, work systems, and written directions in the form of checklists can be a valuable aid in teaching independent self-care skills and household responsibilities. A short list for packing swim gear was written into Adam's schedule on page 47. A checklist to use at bath time was referred to in Catie's schedule on page 46. Catie's bath-time checklist might look like this:

- ☐ Tell Mom **"Mom, I'm ready for the bath water, please."**
- ☐ Undress and put clothes in hamper
- ☐ Choose 4 bath tub toys
- ☐ Get clean washcloth
- ☐ Set the timer for 15 minutes
- ☐ Get in bathtub
- ☐ When timer rings, play time is over - put toys in the bucket.
- ☐ Wash - Mom will help. (On June 1 - Catie starts washing by herself.)
- ☐ Dry body and hang towel on rod
- ☐ Put P.J.'s on
- ☐ Tell Mom **"It's time to check the calendar."**

Several strategies have been built into the checklist to help Catie become more independent. The first and last directions prompt her *to communicate*. Rather than just having a passive role, she is learning to take the initiative to *organize* her evening routine. The checklist prompts her to tell Mom that it is time for the bath water. Notice the specificity in the direction about getting the bath tub toys. It is clear that she cannot dump her entire collection of rubber toys into the bath tub tonight. Within the structure, she takes an active role (setting the timer) and can see exactly what the *expectations are* (when to put toys away.)

Notice the entry about washing. Mom has decided that when the school year is over, she wants Catie to begin to wash herself independently. She knows that it might take a long time and that there will be small steps to take along the way. She also knows that Catie is used to Mom washing her and she might resist or refuse to change the old routine. So, Mom is preparing Catie by showing her when she will start washing herself. Mom writes it on a calendar, too. *(See pages 96-98 about using a calendar.)* When June 1 arrives, Catie will expect a change in the routine, and hopefully experience it with minimal resistance.

On June 1, Catie's mother will write a list or maybe use a sequence of pictures to help Catie learn the steps to follow when washing.

Organizing the work space, supplies, and materials

The location of your student's desk may significantly affect his behavior while working. Try placing his desk to the *side* of the room, away from the door. Some children do better at the *front* of the room. Others feel more comfortable in the *back*. You may need to try a few different locations until determining the best place. Carefully observe your student when deciding where he can most easily learn to work independently. He may be able to tell you, if you ask.

It may be that your student will have one desk. He will set up and take down the cardboard office when needed. Some children work better when there is a *different, permanent* location reserved just for independent work. The office can be permanently set up at a second desk, typically in a quieter location.

There are children who work best when the office is located *outside* of the classroom, either in the hall, in an extra room, or perhaps in a smaller special education classroom. It is not unusual for some special education teachers to renovate an unused *time-out room*, completely changing its purpose. Now it is a distraction-free, well-defined space in which a student can practice independent work. It becomes a "real" office!

Many students with autism have difficulty keeping their school supplies organized. Designate a nearby shelf, table, or counter for the necessary materials, supplies, and books. Label shelves, cupboards, containers, plastic baskets, or trays with what is to be stored inside. Identify and label where completed work is to be put. Color-code folders by subject. Keep pencils in the folders with the work. Label the place where the "office" is to be kept when not in use. Provide and label a spot the schedule is to be kept, if he does not carry it with him.

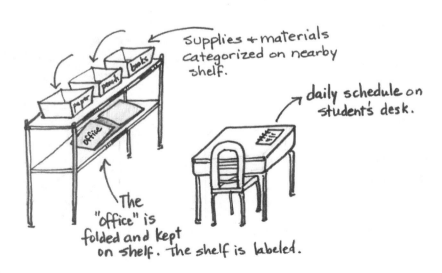

Supplies + materials categorized on nearby shelf.

daily schedule on student's desk.

The "office" is folded and kept on shelf. The shelf is labeled.

197

Modifying worksheets

Assignments come in many forms, depending on the grade level, the skills to be practiced, and teacher preference. Worksheets and related written formats are widely used. For some children with organizational difficulties and problems distinguishing relevant information from details, even the most basic worksheets can be baffling, if not maddening.

Worksheets, workbook pages, and other assignments can be modified in ways that help students become more organized in their approach to working. *Clarify what is important, while minimizing extraneous details.* Rearrange the visual format of worksheets with colored markers, scissors, glue, and the copy machine. Through careful observation of your student, you will learn which types of modifications are most supportive. One of the teacher assistant's jobs can be to make the necessary worksheet modifications for the week. Below you can see a "before and after" example of the same worksheet that has been modified to meet the needs of a particular student.

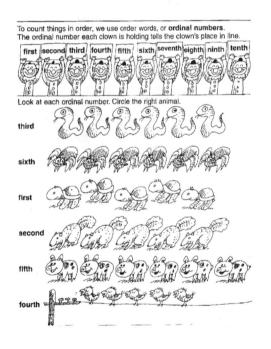

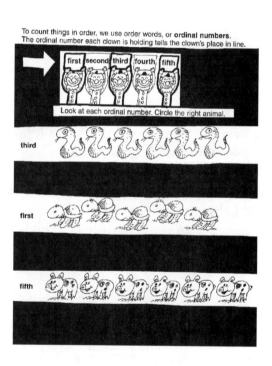

Try these methods when modifying worksheets and other written assignments:

Color-code	Label	Highlight	Limit extra information
Outline	Frame	Underline	Partially filled-in answers
Contrast	Cut out	Enlarge	Circle

Folder Tasks

More structure might be needed for students with significant organizational difficulties and/or students who cannot complete assignments independently because of handwriting difficulties. Actually manipulating and arranging materials in a concrete manner, rather than only writing the correct answer with pen and paper, may elicit greater motivation and cooperation from your student. *Folder tasks* can easily be used for supplementary skill practice.

Folder tasks are made with manilla folders, like those used for filing. Materials such as laminated pictures from magazines, books, workbooks, or textbooks, and flat objects such as plastic counters, puzzle pieces, and cards, make up the raw material for folder tasks. Instead of accomplishing the task by *writing* the answers, the student manipulates the pieces by sorting, matching, or otherwise arranging them to complete the work. The finished work is kept in place, either by slipping the pieces behind paper clips, placing them in pockets, or fastening them in place with Velcro.

Each folder task is self-contained; all the materials required to complete the task are stored in the folder itself. Folder tasks are an excellent alternative to pencil and paper assignments, especially for students with significant organizational and/or handwriting difficulties. Folder tasks are also an excellent alternative to letting your student become too dependent on someone else's assistance with his work. *Folder tasks can be a valuable aid in helping students work independently.* Here is one example of a folder task created to practice reading comprehension and social studies facts. New sentences and new pictures can be added and rearranged to create additional tasks.

Sentences are tucked into the pocket on the left. Student matches the sentences to pictures on the right, by attaching them to the Velcro pieces.

Student satisfaction and motivation

Once the use of structured teaching strategies has become routine, you may find, delightfully, that your child's level of motivation increases along with his independent skills. For many children with autism, the acts of following the list, checking things off as they are accomplished, and "finishing" become motivating and quite satisfying in and of themselves. The systems are predictable and clear. Your child knows what to expect and what will happen when he is finished. It becomes intrinsically motivating to follow the schedule, the work system, and written directions.

Usually, when these visually structured teaching strategies are *properly individualized and used consistently as a dynamic, flexible, and active part of the school day,* systematic reliance on traditional behavior management techniques decrease. Parents and teachers frequently find that they no longer experience the urgent need to use external motivators and "reinforcers" to get the child to work.

Utilizing special interests

A student's satisfaction and motivation increases dramatically when teachers and parents consider his interests. Fascination and devotion to a special interest can open many doors for the student of the creative teacher willing to cultivate what moves him.

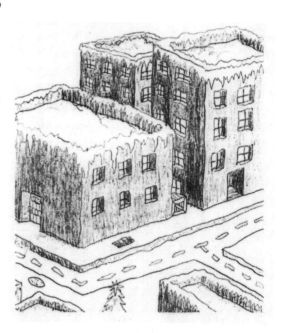

Utilize your child's special interests to capture his attention, introduce new skills, illustrate difficult concepts, motivate and stimulate, increase positive social experiences, and to add overall pleasure and satisfaction to learning. Review the following examples:

1. Allow him to use his special interest when working on an "unrelated" project.

Student's interest:	Buildings
Art project:	Design a Christmas Card
Try:	Allow the student to include his interest in the Christmas Card design. Doug loved drawing buildings. *(See the drawing for a Christmas Card, above, by Doug Buckner, 1991. Notice the hint of a Christmas tree at the bottom of the drawing.)*

2. Introduce a new topic in a way that relates to his special interest.

Student's interest:	Weather
New social studies topic:	Cities, suburbs, and towns in your state
Try:	Record temperatures for designated cities

3. Teach a new or difficult skill by relating it to his special interest.

Student's interest:	Electrical poles and wires
Skill:	Multiplication
Try:	If there were 4 lines attached to the top of an electrical pole, and there were 3 rows of these lines going down the pole, then how many...? *(Present with a drawing.)*

4. Teach abstract concepts by relating them to his special interest.

Student's interest:	Star Trek
Concept:	Empathy and being able to take another person's perspective
Try:	Picard changes form and becomes a foreign entity *(taking another person's perspective).* He now understands what they feel and think *(empathy).*

5. Motivate by allowing the time for special interest when finished working.

Student's interest:	Washing machines
Try:	When work is completed, look through laundromat specialty catalogs

6. Increase social contact through his special interest.

Student's interest:	Years and makes of automobiles
Social skill goal:	Initiate social contact
Try:	Poll classmates, one at a time, as to the types of cars their parents have. Make a chart and share the results with classmates. Then poll classmates as to the type of car they "want." Make another chart, sharing the results.

Outlines, diagrams, models, notes, and mapping

When information must be presented verbally or through lectures, it will help if you augment the lecture with visual aids. Whenever possible, demonstrate concepts with *models, charts, photographs, and pictures.*

✓ **Minimize visual distractions.**

When writing information on the whiteboard or chalkboard, wipe it clean of extraneous information that distracts from what is relevant.

✓ **Use the overhead projector and highlight.**

Display an outline of your presentation and lists of relevant points. Highlight key words with colored markers as you talk. Mind map *(see below)* on the overhead projector.

✓ **Provide written notes.**

Give your student a copy of the lecture notes or an outline of the information you are presenting. Or, arrange with another classmate to duplicate a copy of his or her notes to be shared.

✓ **Try "mind mapping".**

Show how the information fits together, concretely and visually. Mind mapping visually depicts the relationships and connection between the pieces of information.

About mind mapping

Mind mapping is a technique used for planning, organizing, and seeing the connections between concepts or ideas. Variations of mind mapping are also known as clustering, webbing, bubbling, and mapping. They are sometimes referred to as "semantic organizers" or "graphic organizers". Mind mapping can be used for note-taking, to review and remember information, for problem solving, to make plans, and to present information. More information about mind mapping is included in the *Recommended Resources* at the end of this book.

Teachers can provide visual input during verbal presentations and lectures through mind mapping. The mind map highlights and emphasizes the flow of information and *shows how the separate pieces are connected.* For group instruction, use an overhead projector. For individual instruction, use a blank piece of paper and pens while sitting with the student.

Mind mapping has been used with individuals with autism in counseling sessions to help them identify, review, and organize their thoughts; make plans; and help them look at the connections between their ideas, behavior, and desired outcomes. The therapist creates the mind map as the student talks and responds to questions. The mind map serves as the visual focal point during the discussion.

How to mind map

A mind map is created by starting with a main idea or topic, written in the center of the page with a circle drawn around it. Ideas relating to the main idea are written on lines that are drawn outward from the center. Think of the center of the mind map *(the main idea)* as a trunk of a tree. So you are actually adding "branches and stems" *(relevant details)* growing out from the trunk. Each new group of "branches and stems" coming out from the middle should be drawn in the same color. Use a new color for additional ideas that are related to the main theme by creating new branch and stem systems. Mind maps can look many different ways. Here is my mind map *about* mind mapping.

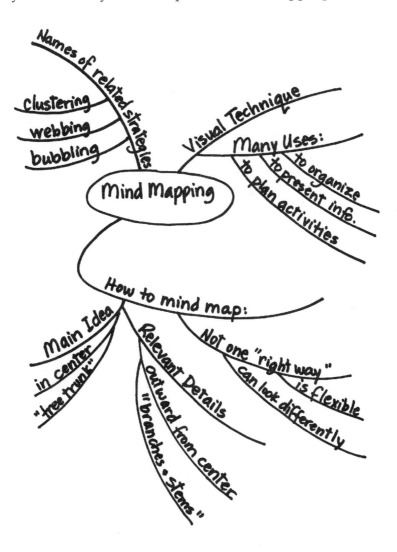

Nine types of lesson adaptations

Cathy Pratt, Director of the Indiana Resource Center for Autism (IRCA) at the Institute for the Study of Developmental Disabilities, promotes the use of educational strategies to support special learners within the general education setting. She has identified the following nine ways to adapt and individualize lessons. They are included here with permission; the IRCA address is listed in the *Recommended Resources* at the end of this book.

Teachers should consider these ideas when they create an individualized program to accommodate their student's learning style, skill level, and interests. Consider the following, if and when appropriate for your student:

1. Size

Adapt the number of items that a learner is expected to learn or complete. For example, *reduce* the number of social studies terms a learner must learn at any one time. Or, in cases where a student has highly developed skills, such as spelling, *increase* the number of spelling words.

2. Time

Adapt the minutes, hours, or days you allow for task completion or testing. For example, increase or decrease the amount of time allotted for an assignment according to your student's pace. For a student working at a slower pace, consider giving him a *head start,* so his work will be due at the same time as the other students' work.

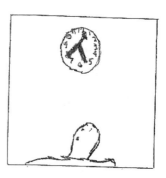

3. Input

Adapt the way information is delivered to the student. For example, use visual structure; plan more concrete examples; provide hands-on activities.

4. Output

Adapt the way the student can respond to instruction. For example, instead of answering questions in writing, allow a verbal response, or allow students to show knowledge by completing *folder tasks* and using other hands-on materials.

5. Difficulty

Adapt the skill level to the student's needs. For example, allow the use of a calculator, simplify directions, break down the steps with *written directions,* or change the rules to accommodate the student's learning style.

6. Participation

Adapt the extent to which the student is actively involved in the task. In geography, have a student hold the globe, while others point out locations. Allow a student to work with a partner, instead of working alone. *Or*, in the case of a student who finds group work confusing or unbearable, allow him to work alone, instead of assigning him to a cooperative group.

7. Level of Support

Increase or decrease the amount of human interaction, as well as providing other types of support, such as visually structured strategies. For example, assign peer buddies, teacher assistants, peer tutors, and small group instruction. Giving your student the support of a *written work system*, instead of relying on a helper or assistant to keep him working, is another way to individualize the level of support.

8. Alternate Goals

Adapt the expectations while using the same materials. For example, in social studies, expect one student to locate just the states while others learn to locate the capitals, as well. Or, expect one student to learn *more* information about a particular subject, especially it is his area of special interest.

9. Substitute or Parallel Curriculum

Provide different instruction and materials to meet a student's individual goals. For example, while most of the students are taking a test, one student is practicing computer skills in the computer lab. Or during German class, the student is engaged in an *independent work session* at his "office".

Group instruction

Expecting a student with autism to participate and benefit from group instruction can be frustrating to both teachers and students. Difficulty knowing where to focus; problems shifting attention; dealing with simultaneous sounds, words, sights, motion, touch, and other sensory stimulation; and weak auditory processing skills combine to make group instruction confusing, bewildering, confusing, or even upsetting to some children. Many children cope by "tuning out".

Careful observation is necessary to determine if and how the student can benefit from group instruction. Try the suggestions that have already been mentioned concerning ways to enhance verbal instruction *(pp. 202-203)*. Typically, a *small* group is better than a large group, and you can give the student a written list using the same four guidelines from the work system *(pp. 172, 194)* to prepare him for what is going to happen. This, of course, becomes more complicated during active group discussions, or when the teacher's spontaneity leads to changes in the plan, on the spot.

In some cases, teachers are often surprised when the student responds to questions with answers that show he *had* been paying attention *(even though it looked like he wasn't)*. Remember what we know about eye contact and autism *(pp. 102, 115)*. It may be easier for your student to pay attention to what is being said when he isn't looking at the speaker. He may also need more time to process (attend, understand, and prepare to respond to) what is being asked. If this is the case with your student, you can try the following:

    Keep a stack of blank index cards and a pen with you.

    As you ask a question, write it on the card. Place it in front of the student and do not repeat the question once you have already asked. He will probably immediately look at what is written (it's visual!). Then wait for his answer. Depending on your student, you might just have to write a few key words.

    You can use the index cards with the entire group, at random.

    The children will see that some of your questions are only spoken, and some of them are paired with a written note. Most of the children will think that it's fun; wondering if and when they will get a card might increase their attention, also.

The computer: *A cautionary measure*

A computer can be a useful tool for children with autism. It can teach and reinforce cognitive skills; be used as an alternative to handwritten assignments; encourage and support communication and social interaction; serve as a leisure activity, a vehicle for creativity, and a good pre-vocational skill. However, when using the computer with your child, do not overlook *one important caution:*

> Your child must learn that there are two kinds of activities with the computer. One, is doing what pleases him *(free time)*. The other is following directions to complete a prescribed task or assignment *(work time)*.

Future vocations with computers may be a real possibility for some children, based on their excellent skills with this technology. However, there are many talented young adults with autism, with computer expertise, who are unable to come close to getting a job using this talent. Why?

It is because over the years, the computer was primarily used as a free-time or leisure activity. It had become a routine so ingrained that he is *unable to do what someone else wants him to do on the computer*. The combination of the computer being a compelling special interest, and the long-established routine of doing what he wants, makes for an extremely inflexible and difficult habit to break when there are specific job requirements in the office or other workplace. From his point of view, it just might not make sense.

Especially if your child is highly skilled on the computer, it is imperative that he learn from the very beginning that there is computer work time and computer free time; and that he engage in both *(page 177)*. This can

be indicated clearly on his daily schedule. As he matures, give him a variety of jobs and assignments to do, lots of different directions to follow, doing things not necessarily of his own choosing. This will help expand the ways he is able to use his talent; and help him become more flexible. You are keeping the door open for a possible future vocation with computers. It might be too late if you wait until he is older and has already established rigid habits.

In the situation of an adolescent who is skilled on the computer, but cannot stand to do what someone else wants him to do, realize that he has a wonderful leisure skill, but acknowledge the fact that he probably will not be unable to use this skill vocationally, *even if he is very talented*. **We have found that the most successful vocational training for individuals with autism begins in childhood.**

Homework

As clarified in the workbook on page 183, there must be a clear distinction made between work that is meant to be completed independently, and work that requires help. *With this in mind, teachers must have input from parents about what happens at home. Teachers and parents should work as a team to ensure that homework is a positive learning experience.* Try the following suggestions that are appropriate:

- Allow your child to **take a break** immediately after arriving home from school. Refrain from asking questions about the day and making demands, right away. Give him space and quiet time.

- Provide a written **after-school schedule**. The activities should be appropriate for your child's age, interests, and needs. Include ample quiet time and time for being alone, for favorite snacks and activities, as well as scheduling in chores and homework. Alternate unappealing activities with favorite ones. *(Pp. 45 and 46)*

- Before leaving school, your child should get the homework assignment list from the teacher. **Do not insist that the *child* write this list, unless he can do it independently and easily.** For many, the act of copying down the assignments from the board is too difficult, overwhelming, and frustrating. This may not be a priority right now.

- At home, you can modify the assignment list to create a **work system for homework**. Remember to add what he will do after finishing at the end of the list. *(Review pages 172, 183, and 194.)*

- If not included already, add **written directions** for specific assignments *(pp.195-196)*.

- Keep a record of how long it takes your child to complete his homework. Communicate with the teacher and compare it with the standard amount of time that his classmates typically spend on homework. If there is a significant difference, assignments should be modified appropriately. **Consider further timing modifications to meet your individual child's needs for more or less homework.**

- Keep a **duplicate set of textbooks** at home if other organizational methods (checklists, routines, backpack) don't help.

What are the *most important* skills I should teach?

There are many different subject areas, curriculum guides, courses of study, and educational philosophies. Schools have their own guidelines while individual teachers and parents have their own biases and opinions. Each student comes with particular strengths, interests, and needs. There is limited time in the school day, and there is a lot to do.

The TEACCH Program works with children, adolescents, and adults, who have been educated in very different settings; from home-schools, private schools, self-contained special education classrooms, resource programs, and full-time general-education settings. We see the kinds of skills these adolescents and adults have, by the time they leave school and enter the job market. With this long-range view, we are constantly able to evaluate educational programs based on how it realistically will affect the lives of adults with autism.

No matter how skilled and talented your child may be, or how much knowledge he possesses; if he is inflexible and cannot handle change; if he is disorganized and requires constant prompts; if he obsesses on certain topics and cannot switch his attention; if he cannot follow directions or becomes resistant or angry when he is told what to do; he will sooner or later fail to keep a job.

Simply stated, by the time a child reaches adulthood, it is critical that he has learned to be organized; to function *(work and play)* independently; to use his strengths and skills in a positive and/or productive manner; to communicate effectively; and to have a method of understanding what might be confusing to him.

☑ The schedule and other structured strategies play a crucial role in adult life, and on the job, for most working adolescents and adults with autism.

Review the introductory information about the schedule *(pp. 36-49).* When it used dynamically and consistently, the schedule can help your child become more flexible; stay organized and involved; monitor obsessions or time focused on special interests; handle leisure time; follow directions and work independently; soften resistance to authority; and get along with others more easily. *These are the life skills and vocational behaviors he must have in the workplace!*

If a high functioning child has been educated *without becoming proficient in using a schedule or other types of structured strategies,* he very often will not have the tools which help him function successfully and independently when dealing with the daily—and overwhelmingly complicated—demands of work and private life *no matter how smart he is.*

A job provides more than a paycheck. The workplace is an important source of daily social contact. How many of us actually spend *more* time with our co-workers than with our families and friends? And sometimes co-workers become friends. The constancy of a job often fulfills many *social* needs, too.

☑ The most effective vocational and life-skills training starts when a child with autism is young.

Incorporate the schedule and other structured teaching strategies daily. *Use them in creative and flexible ways, in a multitude of settings, at home and at school.* Teach your child that checklists are meaningful tools by using them often. Even though it sounds simplistic, your child's ability to use checklists independently can have long-lasting, significant, and overall positive effects on his adult life—more than most other skills he might learn in school. When planning his educational program, make sure that you:

- Review the results of formal and informal assessment.

- Consider his innate style of learning.

- Capitalize on his natural gifts and strengths.

- Pay attention to his greatest needs.

- Determine educational goals based on the above...

- **...and teach your child to independently use and follow a schedule, work system, and written directions.** *(See pages 36-49, 167, 171-173, and 194-196.)*

More educational interventions

Happily, a growing awareness has emerged over the last few years, and excellent resources of teaching methods and educational interventions especially for high functioning students with autism have been published. In these books, you will find variations of the ideas in this book, as well as other ideas that may fit your child. Review the *Recommended Resources* at the end of this book. Read the articles about educational strategies that are posted on Asperger Syndrome Web sites and the TEACCH Web site.

Always remember to try to see the world through your child's perspective, individualizing whatever strategies you try. Reread page **xiv**, at the beginning of this book, about the "keys to keep in mind".

The quiet area

As mentioned in Chapter 3, the *quiet area* can provide a welcome respite from the demands, frustrations, and overwhelm which accompany daily life for

many children with autism. Identify a spot for the quiet area which will work for the teacher, the student with autism, and the rest of the class. It may be a corner in the classroom, a designated place in the hall, or in another room. One adult said that it would have made a big difference in school,

"if I could have been allowed to go somewhere where it was quiet, when it got to be too much, so I could have gotten calmed down...that would have helped."

A concern of some teachers is how to justify this special area for one student and not for others. Ordinarily, all it takes is a matter-of-fact statement, "John needs to take a quiet break once in a while in order to stay focused and calm." Children will accept an explanation that is simple, clear, and honest. Two positive results of the quiet area can be:

1. Prevention

One, by including time for the quiet area on his schedule throughout the day, you help to prevent overwhelm, which otherwise can snowball into distress and anxiety. The distribution of quiet area times on the schedule should be determined through careful observation and informal assessment. Some children might only need one visit to the quiet area all day. Others might need frequent periods of respite, as many as four to six short visits throughout the day. You may discover that your student benefits from a routine visit to the quiet area *before* or *after* a particular activity. An individual child's needs often fluctuate, depending on individual circumstances.

2. Self-awareness

Two, through consistency and familiarity with the quiet area, and growing awareness by the child as to the purpose of the quiet area, he may learn more about himself. Hopefully, over time, he will learn how to take care of himself, before "melt down" occurs. Your student may learn to gauge his need for respite, and know what to do about it. He may learn to estimate, at the beginning of the day, how frequently or when he might need the quiet area. In this case, happily adapt his schedule accordingly.

Other strategies to help relieve and prevent anxiety will be discussed in Chapter 11.

Why is he like that?

Some parents are hesitant to talk directly with other students and significant people at school about the fact that their child has autism or Asperger Syndrome. Most parents do not want the child to be thought of as different. Maybe if the differences are not mentioned, then the child will be "just like every other child." Or, perhaps by not mentioning them, the differences will be minimized.

Of course the ultimate goal is that every individual is respected and appreciated, with all of our personal quirks and uniqueness. Our challenge is,  though, how do we make this happen? How do we create an environment of mutual respect where every child's humanity is embraced and celebrated? How do we create an environment where "difference makes no difference anymore," as stated so eloquently in the opening quote of this book?

The truth is that even if the teacher or parent does not point out to your child's classmates that your child has autism, or simply that he is different in certain ways, they already know it. But, they don't know why. As a result, the other children typically fill in the *missing* information with *wrong* information. (*"He must be crazy/stupid/weird..."*) Consequently, behaviors ranging from ignoring and whispering, to name-calling and other overtly rude or hurtful actions, sometimes result. The classmates' responses largely depend on the particular combination of your child's unique traits, the age of the children, and the general classroom climate.

There is an alternative. It is education.

Programs to teach peers about differences

Uncensored questions and honest answers can lay the groundwork for understanding, empathy, and acceptance. Since 1985, this author has spoken with over a thousand students from kindergarten through high school about their peers with autism and other differences from the norm. In almost every instance, an immediate positive change in attitude was observed following the presentations. Among a few students, there sprouted long-term interest and understanding of the child with autism. The program *Understanding Friends* was created by this author for the purpose of educating peers about differing abilities found in every person. It is a simple program which can be adapted to all grade levels, and individualized to explain autism as it relates to a particular classmate. The children learn that even though all people are different in a multitude of ways, we are all the same in one major way; that we deserve to be understood and accepted for who we are.

Understanding Friends begins with an introduction in which the class explores how everyone is unique. Then the children rotate between experiential centers which are set up to simulate "different abilities": fine motor, visual, sensory, perceptual, and auditory processing differences. Afterward, the term *autism* can be introduced, and questions and answers about their peer with autism follow. Often, the program concludes by reading a related children's book. Questions are encouraged and the mystery about the "different" peer shifts to understanding. A lesson plan for presenting *Understanding Friends* can be found on the TEACCH Web site. *(See Recommended Resources at the end of this book.)*

The Sixth Sense was developed by Carol Gray as a way to explain why some people have difficulty with social understanding. It is a short presentation, which begins with a discussion about the five senses and introduces the concept of the "social sense" as the sixth sense. The ability to take another person's perspective is defined as this social sense. This program is meant to be used with children from third grade and up, and is an effective way to explain autism to groups of adults as well. The lesson plan for presenting *The Sixth Sense* can be found in the booklet, *Taming the Recess Jungle,* by Carol Gray, as listed in the *Recommended Resources* at the end of this book.

Susan Moreno, in her booklet **High-Functioning Individuals With Autism: Advice and Information for Parents and Others Who Care**, published by MAAP, describes a way to *simulate sensory processing problems,* common to many individuals with autism. Using a strobe light, radio, gloves with different textures, and verbal directions, typical students experience what it might feel like to receive confusing or distorted sensory information. Information about this booklet can be found in the *Recommended Resources*, under MAAP (More Able Autistic People).

Talking about autism and your child

A formal program is not necessary in order to talk with peers about your child. Your willingness to invite open discussion and to answer questions is the key. Keep your explanations simple, open, direct, matter-of-fact, and reassuring. Information from the pages of this workbook can help you plan your talk. Most children *want* to understand, and when they do, the transformative power of education is realized.

Depending on the ages and maturity of your child and the class at large, it is often better to arrange for your child to be out of the classroom during these presentations or discussions. Classmates are more apt to ask the questions that are on their minds if their peer with autism is not in the room. In most cases, depending on your child, he should be told that there is going to be a presentation about autism (or *differences*, or whatever term you use). Usually the child himself prefers not to be present, although he might want to hear "what happened" when it is all over.

In those cases where the child *chooses* to be there, it is imperative that he know ahead of time what is going to happen and what is going to be said. If your child is going to be present, he should already have an understanding about autism and how it affects him personally. The program should *not* be his first introduction to autism. If he is to be present, he should probably already feel secure about having autism. In this case, he may even want to answer some of his class-mates' questions himself.

If you are a teacher who wants to educate your students about autism and how it relates to their classmate, it goes without saying that it must be done with the full permission of the child's parents. Depending on the age and level of understanding of the child, it may be desirable to have his permission as well. There may be individual situations where it may not feel right yet, to a particular family or child. Even beyond the ethics of confidentiality, which obviously apply here, it is imperative that the desires of those parents and children who are hesitant to share such personal information with others, must be respected.

Chapter 10: Friends

Workbook

What Is a Friend?

A friend is a person who is not in my family, but is **important** to me.

A friend is a person who is special because we like each other. A friend spends time with me. We have fun together. We like to do many of the **same things**.

I will ⬭circle⬭ or highlight what is true for me. 🖉

- ▶ I do not have friends.
- ▶ I wish that I had a friend.
- ▶ I do not want a friend.
- ▶ I have one friend. My friend's name is_____ .
- ▶ I have many friends. Their names are: _____

_____ .

- ▶ Other: _____

These are the things that I like to do with a friend:

1. _____

2. _____

3. _____

4. _____

Playing With Friends

Some children like to spend a lot of time with friends, playing and talking. Some children like to play by themselves. **I will mark what is true for me.** ✎

1.   I like to:

   ▶ play with one friend at a time.

   ▶ play with a group of friends at the same time.

   ▶ play by myself.

   ▶ sometimes play with friends and sometimes by myself.

2.   I mostly like to:

   ▶ play with boys.

   ▶ play with girls.

   ▶ play with children who are younger than me.

   ▶ play with children who are older than me.

   ▶ play with children who are about the same age as me.

   ▶ play with adults.

   ▶ play with _____ (name of person)

3.   When I am with friends, I like to:

   ▶ play by myself, but in the same room as my friends.

   ▶ watch my friends play, but not get too involved.

   ▶ at first watch my friends play, and then join in later on.

   ▶ play together with my friends most of the time.

   ▶ not be with them at all; I would rather play by myself.

Pretend Play

Most children like to pretend. **Pretending** is when children say that they are not themselves. They might talk in a different voice. They might say that they are someone else. They know that it is **not real**, but most children think that pretending is fun.

Many children with autism do not like to pretend.

I will (circle) or highlight what is true for me. 🖉

- ▶ I do not like to pretend.
- ▶ I don't know how to pretend.
- ▶ I think that pretending is silly or useless.
- ▶ I wish I could pretend.
- ▶ Pretending is not fun for me. I like to play in other ways.
- ▶ The ways I like to play are: _____ .

Some children with autism *do* like to pretend. They might imagine a fantasy world and pretend they are in it. If I like to pretend, I will mark what is true for me about pretending. 🖉 (If I do not like to pretend, I do not have to read more on this page.)

- ▶ I like to pretend.
- ▶ I usually like to pretend by myself.
- ▶ I usually like to pretend with other children.
- ▶ I want other children to imagine *my same* fantasy world.
- ▶ I like to get *new pretend ideas* from other children.
- ▶ other:_____

Playing Outside

Most children like to play outside. There are many things to do outside.

I will ⬭circle or highlight what I like to do. ✎

I like being *active*, like:

- ▶ playing on playground equipment; swings, slides, climbing bars, _____ .
- ▶ throwing and catching a ball
- ▶ shooting baskets
- ▶ riding a bike
- ▶ jumping rope
- ▶ playing hopscotch
- ▶ roller skating or roller blading
- ▶ doing cartwheels or somersaults
- ▶ running
- ▶ other: _____

I like being *quiet and less active*, like:

- ▶ sitting still
- ▶ lying down
- ▶ listening to birds and other sounds
- ▶ watching small things like grass or insects
- ▶ walking around
- ▶ playing in a sandbox or digging in the ground
- ▶ other: _____

Friends

Running and Other Motor Skills

Running is a big part of many games. Running is called a **motor skill**. The word *motor* refers to our ability to move.

Some children have good motor skills. It means that they can run, jump, climb, hop, throw, catch, and move quickly, easily, and smoothly. They have good balance and coordination.

Running, jumping, throwing, and catching might be difficult for some children. They might not be able to move quickly or smoothly. Their bodies might move in ways that look "floppy" or "stiff".

Some children with autism have very good motor skills, but many children with high functioning autism or Asperger Syndrome have difficulty with motor skills.

I will circle or highlight what is true for me. 🖉

- ▶ I can run and jump easily.
- ▶ It is easy for me to throw and catch a ball.
- ▶ I do not usually bump into things, or trip and fall down.
- ▶ It is hard to throw and catch a ball.
- ▶ I have difficulty running and jumping easily.
- ▶ I often bump into things, or trip and fall down.
- ▶ I like to run.
- ▶ I do not like to run.
- ▶ other: _____

Winning and Losing

Many games end with winning or losing. Usually only one player or one team can win the game. The other players lose that particular game.

Most children like to win. They might get angry or sad when they are losing. When children play a game and get very, very, angry, they are being **bad sports.** Being a bad sport is when a child yells, says bad words, throws a piece of equipment, tries to hit someone, or does something else that is not polite. Bad sports ruin the game. It is not good to ruin the game.

Many children think that they should win all the time. They think that winning is right. They think that losing is wrong. That's why they get upset if they do not win.

But it is impossible for the same person to win all the time. A wise person once said *"I win some, and I lose some!"* Winning and losing is part of being human.

Winning and losing is *not the same* as good and bad.

Good sports can lose a game and still be good. I can try to be a good sport when I win *and* lose.

Being a good sport is the *right* way to play.

Friends

Being a Good Sport

A good sport is a person who tries to play the game as best as he can. At the end of the game he might win or he might lose. Good sports do not yell bad words, throw equipment, try to hit someone, or _____ .

How to Be A Good Sport

People like to play with good sports. I can practice being a good sport. I will say **"Good Game!"** at home with my family while I shake their hands. We can repeat what a wise person once said,

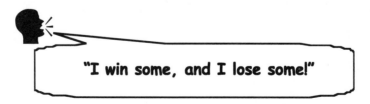

Teams

Some games are played with **teams**. Teams are groups of children who play together, against another team.

Some teams have only a few children. Some teams have many children.

Games and sports that require the team members to play all together can be difficult for many children with autism. **I will mark what is true for me.** ✎

Playing on teams might be confusing to me because:

▶ I don't remember who is on my team.

▶ I don't really understand what to do.

▶ There is too much going on at the same time.

▶ I have difficulty throwing, catching, or running.

▶ other: _____

Some children with autism have more fun if they participate in *individual sports.* They might be on a team, but the team members do not have to play all together at the same time. I might like to try:

▶ swimming

▶ cross country or track

▶ skating

▶ bicycling

▶ chess

▶ other: _____

A Friend Coming to My House

Playing with friends is fun for most children. But there are some children who have *more fun being alone.*

Some children with autism want to have friends, but *don't know how to make friends.* Or they may try to play with a friend, but it is not very fun.

I will (circle) or highlight what is true for me. ✏

- ▶ I want to go to a friend's house.
- ▶ I would rather play by myself at home.
- ▶ I want to have a friend come to my house. I can get ready by following this checklist:

☐ Invite a friend to my house for an hour or two.

☐ Before my friend comes, my parent and I can make a list of the things we can do. (Including a snack!)

☐ Some of the things on the list can be my special interests and some of the things can be my friend's special interests.

☐ My friend and I will take turns choosing from the list, what we will do. We can spend 10 minutes on each choice. (Or another time that is equal.)

☐ Or, ahead of time, my parent can make a schedule for my friend and I to follow.

☐ The last thing we do will be my friend's choice, because he is a guest at my house.

Getting Along With a Friend

A friend usually does not make fun of me. He or she is nice to me. I try to be **nice** to my friend, too.

I like my friend, but sometimes we might not agree. I might get angry with my friend. My friend might get angry with me. *We might want to do different things.*

But friends do not stay angry with each other for a long time and we will probably want to play together again.

We can do something to make it easier to play with each other without getting angry a lot. We can try to *get along* with each other. We can follow this checklist:

☐ 1. If we argued, say "I apologize" or "I'm sorry".
☐ 2. Then say "Let's play together again".
☐ 3. We can write a list of the things I like to do.
☐ 4. We can write a list of the things my friend likes to do.
☐ 5. We will circle the things on the lists that match; the things we both like to do.
☐ 6. Write a new list: *"The Things We Want To Do Together"*

If there are things that I want to do, but my friend does not want to do, that is OK. *I can do those things later by myself or with someone else.* Good friends learn to get along.

Friends

I Wonder Why...

There are some things that I don't understand about other children. *I wonder why they do the things that they do.*

Here is a list of the things that I do not understand. Why do other children do these things?

1. Why does _____ ?

2. Why does _____ ?

3. Why does _____ ?

4. Why does _____ ?

5. Why does _____ ?

6. Why does _____ ?

7. Why does _____ ?

8. Why does _____ ?

Friends

Should Friends Know About Autism?

Friends might not understand some of the things I do or some of the things I say.

**Having autism affects me,
and it also affects my friends.**

My friend might *understand me better* if he or she knows about autism. Then I might understand my friend, too.

My parent can help me figure out which friends should know about autism and me.

We think these friends should know about autism and me:

1 _____   4 _____

2 _____   5 _____

3 _____   6 _____

See Chapter 9 for information about teaching other children about autism.

Friends

A Mentor Is a Special Kind of Friend

A **mentor** is a special kind of friend. A mentor is older than me, usually an adult. *A mentor is an adult who likes me and the same things that I like.* Spending time with a mentor is easy and fun.

A mentor can be a good friend to a child with autism, especially as the child grows into adulthood.

- A mentor can help me learn more about myself and help me learn more about the world.
- A mentor can try to answer questions and help me find the answers.
- A mentor can encourage me with my hopes and dreams and can help me find good ways to use my talents, skills, and special interests.

Maybe I will have a mentor when I am older. A mentor is usually not my parent, but my parent can help me find a mentor. *A mentor might be a teacher, a friend of my parent, an aunt, an uncle, or someone else.*

I will mark what is true for me. ✎

- ▶ I would like to have a mentor when I am older.
- ▶ I already have someone who is like a mentor. This person's name is _____ .
- ▶ other: _____

For Parents and Teachers

"If the point of social interaction is to have it be a positive experience, to feel better as a result of it—not worse, then finding what works for me and doing that tends to do the trick."

–Dave Spicer, on social situations

Ideas in This Chapter

✓ Something to think about

✓ Assessment

✓ Identify what is fun from your child's perspective

✓ Assess his level of social interaction

✓ Provide the necessary structure

✓ The equation for a successful social experience

✓ Buddies, peer helpers, and other partnerships

✓ Individualizing the social event: A big party is not always big fun!

✓ Social Stories and Comic Strip Conversations

✓ We are all in this together

✓ True friends

✓ Social groups: getting to know others with autism

Something to think about

The subject of friends can be a sensitive issue for parents of children with high functioning autism. It can be painful to watch other children in the neighborhood playing and building friendships with ease and spontaneity. It is so effortless, compared to your child's hesitation, awkwardness, resistance, or

downright failures. Difficulties in the area of socialization are primary for children and adults with autism. And, while many individuals with autism struggle with this issue, it is important to remember what one young woman with autism told me to pass on to the participants of an upcoming teacher training,

"Tell them not to judge the degree of my happiness by what makes them happy. Tell them that I like to be alone."

First, and above all, we need to respect the desires of our children. A situation that may be upsetting you about your child's social life may not matter one bit to him.

On the other hand, we can help our children make sense out of the complex social arena by adding structure to shared activities that could develop into a fun social experience. By doing this, we are giving them the freedom to enjoy social activities that would otherwise be unpredictable and stressful.

Assessment

Just as in other areas of your child's development, successful acquisition of social skills must start with a realistic and objective assessment. Consider the following three key principles which are introduced in TEACCH trainings when talking about social development: identify what is fun for your child, assess his current level of social interaction, and provide the structure that is needed for him to be successful and to have fun. These three assessment areas are

discussed below. (TEACCH training programs are posted on the TEACCH Web site, listed in the *Recommended Resources* at the end of this book.)

Identify what is fun from your child's perspective

Being together with other children is fun for most "typical" children. Social contact can immediately transform a boring day into a fun time. It is probably different for your child with autism. Simply getting your child together with others may not necessarily be fun for him. When teachers and parents want to increase successful social opportunities for their child with autism, they must first recognize what is truly fun for their child. What does *he* consider enjoyable? What *captures* his attention? What *sustains* his attention? What does he *do for fun*?

Remember, just because an activity is thought of as fun for most children does not necessarily mean that it will automatically be fun for your child.

Assessment #1: What is fun?

Make a list of what he enjoys. Don't stop at the obvious *(computer, drawing, etc.)* and notice the little things. What gets his attention while looking out the car window? What pictures does he stop at when leafing through magazines? What was he doing or looking at when you heard him laugh? What does he like to look at? What textures or actions feel good to him? When you notice something that captures his attention, even for a moment, remember what it was and jot it down on this list.

_____

_____

_____

_____

_____

_____

_____

Assess his level of social interaction

Just as the introduction and teaching of new cognitive skills starts with an accurate assessment of mastered and emerging skills, so must the teaching of skills in the area of social development. *At what level is your child most comfortable? What levels of social interaction has he mastered?*

While most children typically master each of the following steps before entering kindergarten, it is not uncommon for individuals with autism to be most comfortable at one of the more basic levels, even into adulthood. Read the following list and note the levels of social interaction which are most natural, spontaneous, enjoyable, and relaxing to him.. *What does he do, with whom, without your prodding? What are his current levels of spontaneous social interaction?*

1. Proximity

Is your child able to tolerate the presence of others close to him while he is playing? A young child who is emerging or has mastered this level is one who will stay in the same area as others while he plays. No interaction is necessary, but he enjoys playing when others are around. If he consistently moves away when others come near, he may be indicating that he is not yet achieved comfort at this level. An adult with autism once remarked that

"I might be awkward in the company of people....but I enjoy proximity even if I'm not interacting. I like being near others."

2. Looking

Does your child notice others and what others are doing? Does he look or glance at others while they are playing? Is he interested in watching what others are doing?

3. Parallel Play

Does your child play alongside others who are engaged in their own, but similar, activity? *An adult with autism pointed out that this is the level at which he is consistently most comfortable. Taking a quiet walk with someone or jogging alongside another person are the social activities he finds most enjoyable.*

4. Sharing

Is your child comfortable sharing materials or toys while he is playing? Is he willing to let others play with "his" toys?

5. Cooperative

Is your child able to play together with another child or a group of children, using the same materials or toys, at the same time? Examples of cooperative play are completing a floor puzzle with someone else, pulling clay for building from a common lump of clay, building a large structure with other children in the block center, or making cookies with the same cookie cutters and dough.

6. Turn Taking

Does your child understand about turns? Is he able to follow the sequence and anticipate when it is his turn and when it is someone else's turn? Does he take turns willingly?

7. Rules

Traditional table-top games, as well as physical games played in the gym or outside, are organized by rules. Does your child understand and follow the rules in relationship to other players? How about unwritten rules of playing on the playground or in the neighborhood? One man with autism remarked that, as a child, "everyone seemed to know what to do, and I did not".

Assessment #2: Level of social interaction

Try to be an objective observer of your child. Look over the seven levels again, and answer these questions about him, *at this current time:*

What level(s) are most difficult?

_____

What level(s) of interaction does he enjoy the most, without having problems?

_____

At what level(s) is he most comfortble?

_____

Circle your answers to the last two questions.

After you have assessed (1) what is fun for your child and (2) what is your child's current level, or levels, of social interaction, then you are ready to determine (3) the structure your child needs for the particular social activity.

Provide the necessary structure

Look carefully at the specific social situation through the eyes of your child. How does he know what to do, where to stand, when it starts, how long it will last, when it is done, what to expect from the other person, etc? Be aware of the type and degree of stimulation in the environment. Try to imagine how your child might experience the situation through his eyes and his sensory world.

Add structure where necessary for your child. You might consider setting up the activity in a quiet room, away from extraneous loud or distractng activities. Use his schedule so he will be able to anticipate *when the activity will*

begin and what will occur when it is over. Written directions organize the activity by *breaking down the steps and showing the sequence*. Visual structure such as labeling, color coding, a turn-taking card, and visual markers will clarify other assumptions: *where to stand, whose turn it is, where to put objects, and what happens where*. Perhaps communication cue cards would take the stress out of knowing *what to say* at certain times.

Take the guesswork out of the situation for him, as much as possible. Do what is necessary by adding structure to create a successful experience, so it will be fun...*and he may just want to do it again!*

Assessment #3: Structure

Imagine yourself from another culture, or even another planet. What kinds of questions would you have about the social situation? Notice what "everyone assumes" about it, observe your child, and try to imagine it from his perspective. Ask these types of questions:

- Where am I supposed to stand/sit/move?
- Is it my turn?
- What do I do next?
- How long will this last? Is it done?
- Why is it so loud/hot/cold/itchy/busy/distracting...here?
- Where can I go to get away from the noise, etc?

Add *structure* to clarify, simplify, and make easier. Write *social stories* to build understanding about specific issues.

Now you are ready to put all the assessment information together. →

The equation for a successful social experience

Keep the three key principles in mind, and refer to this equation to guide you in planning social activities for your child.

What is fun for your child +

His social comfort level +

Structure = Social Success

Your plan:

At home, consider these ideas when planning your child's next birthday party or family gathering. At school, remember these principles when writing "social goals". Set up the social situation using information you noted in the three assessments:

1. Something that is fun for your child: _____

2. Currently, his most comfortable and enjoyable social level: _____

3. Specific structure that helps: _____

_____

_____

_____

How will you set up the particular social situation you have in mind, using the *equation for a successful social experience?*

_____

_____

_____

For a discussion on the importance of *success*, refer to page 34.

Buddies, peer helpers, and other partnerships

Many years ago at the Chapel Hill TEACCH Center, the therapists identified some of the common roles played by friends at school. By reviewing these roles, we can get ideas of ways to help identify "buddies" for children with autism to facilitate the development of friendships. According to your child's needs and the school environment, consider identifying a peer or peers to fulfill one or more of these roles.

1. Peer tutor
2. Lunch partner
3. Companion for "specials" such as art, music...
4. Free-time buddy
5. Extracurricular buddy (school clubs, etc.)
6. Homework partner
7. Project partner
8. Travel companion (bus, walking home)
9. Neighborhood buddy

The success of these relationships usually depends on both children having interests and experiences in common, as well as the peer's willingness to understand and empathize with your child, and your child's authentic desire for companionship. *Teach the peer ahead of time, how to use any structured strategies that are in place for your child.* Help the peer understand how autism affects your child, in both positive and negative ways. You may want to reread the information about explaining autism to peers on pages 187, 212-214.

Keep in mind that for many children with autism, one peson to be with at a time, is best!

Individualizing the social event: "A big party is not always big fun!"

The widely accepted practice of providing a child with plenty of social opportunities by including him in a large group of peers, may only result in further isolation. Close observation of your child before, during, and after spending time in a large group may reveal that inclusion in the large group may not be very fun from his point of view. *If this is true,* being in large groups of children for extended periods of time could possibly *hinder* your child's social development rather than support it.

When most people find themselves invited to a social event which might be awkward or aversive, the natural inclination is to avoid attending the event, or at the least, plan to go home early! Why would it be any different for a child with autism who struggles with the social aspects of life all the time? Since social relatedness is a core area of difficulty for children with autism, it is imperative that the methods used to help the acquisition of social skills are very structured and thoughtful. It must be more than simply making sure he is physically "part of the group."

You might discover that a regularly scheduled, structured activity with *one* peer will offer your child the most enjoyment, confidence, and desire for future social interaction. In contrast to struggling or withdrawing in a large group of children, he may actually relax and begin to have fun when he is in a simpler, more structured situation. Try both and ask him which he prefers.

A next step might be to merge the structured one-to-one activity *into* the larger group. This would only take place after success and mastery is accomplished first in the quieter, smaller, or more structured environment.

By acknowledging and respecting the child's sensory, cognitive, motor, communicative, and social differences, we can see that small steps, built on the principles of fun, comfort, predictability, order, familiarity, and individual preference, will nourish real social success.

Social Stories and Comic Strip Conversations

As introduced on page 98, social stories can be written to clarify problematic social situations. Comic Strip Conversations (*p. 129*) can be a useful tool to help the parent or teacher discover the child's perspective about what is happening or what has taken place.

Social stories are written in a matter-of-fact, reassuring manner from the child's point of view. Through his eyes, the story describes *another* perspective– that of neurotypical, or "non-autistic" children or adults. By giving the child more information, the targeted social situation may begin to make sense to him.

Write social stories for your child when his behavior indicates that there is something he does not understand, *but also to acknowledge success.* Carol Gray strongly encourages us to write many many social stories that acknowledge the good things that our children are doing so they learn more directly and specifically, and their self-esteem can be nurtured. See Carol Gray's publications, listed in the *Recommended Resources* at the end of this book, for instructional information.

We are all in this together

Besides promoting social success by considering what is fun, assessing your child's level of social comfort, adding visual structure, encouraging buddies, and writing social stories, there is another essential component in promoting successful social functioning.

Help the other important adults and children in your child's life rethink their automatic interpretations of your child's behavior which aren't necessarily true. Commonly held judgments, like "he must not like me because he is not looking at me," or "he is not having fun because he is by himself," may not always apply.

Help the key people in your child's life understand that autism causes differences that can't always be interpreted accurately by typical social rules and assumptions. Show them this book and let them see what you and your child have marked on the pages.

Help them learn what they can *change about themselves* in order to be a better friend to your child. Help them identify what *they* do that may be confusing to their peer with autism. It is not only the job of the child with autism to change and learn. Friendship, by definition, is a mutual and reciprocal relationship, therefore the changing, learning, and understanding must also be reciprocal. *We are all in this together!*

True friends

There probably are people in your child's life who find him, just the way he is, to be a wonderful and fascinating individual. There will probably be others who will feel the same way in the future. As he grows, help him appreciate,

enjoy, and care about these people. In the coming years, find a mentor, someone in addition to you or your spouse, who will be there for him as he grows into adulthood. Meaningful reciprocity between your child and others will develop its own form that may look different from the outside, but will be sincere and true in its own way.

Social groups: getting to know others with autism

For many years, TEACCH therapists and directors across the state of North Carolina have organized social groups for children, teenagers, and adults with autism. In many areas, parent groups organize social groups for their children. The groups vary in make-up and purpose, depending on the range of abilities, needs, desires, and functioning levels of their members. In the very beginning, many of us who facilitated social groups concentrated on the teaching and development of social skills as a primary focus of these groups, with the secondary (but still important) purpose of having fun. Over the years, as familiarity grows and relationships among group members emerge over time, the priorities have shifted. Fellowship and fun has taken the lead.

The make-up of the groups is sometimes balanced between children with autism and typically-developing peers, or in the case of adults, participation with volunteers from local colleges and the community at large. In some situations, though, these regular events have evolved into social gatherings made up almost exclusively of and for people with autism. According to many members of social groups for adults with high functioning autism or Aspergers, they feel more relaxed within this group than they are "outside" the group. Some group members talk about the comfort, reassurance, and self-validity that is felt while together. Perhaps as a consequence, increased social spontaneity emerges in delightful ways. *Humor and self-expression, both commonly thought of as lacking in autism, abound! Fun, pure and simple!*

As your child matures, consider starting a social group for peers with high functioning autism and Aspergers. It might be based on common interests, like a social group for teenagers in Asheville, North Carolina. The members, along with TEACCH therapists and adult volunteers with autism, met in a group to explore computers, computer games, the Internet, creating Web pages, and other related high-interest activities. As group members got to know one another, the activities broadened and expanded into non-computer-related activities as well.

Another variation of a social group was one organized to bring together teenagers who had high functioning autism or Asperger Syndrome with their adult counterparts. This group's focus was two-fold; to discuss problem issues encountered by the teenagers *and* to provide a social event. What made this group unique was that the TEACCH therapist facilitated the discussion in partnership with the adults with autism, whose distinctive perspective of having "been there and survived it" was reassuring to the younger members.

Social groups for younger children consist of activities appropriate to the age level, interests, and desires of the members. Social groups for older children, teenagers and adults have enjoyed the following activities. Remember to use structure on an individual basis to insure understanding and enjoyment. Add to the idea list by including the group members' interests, even if the interests might be considered unusual by ordinary standards.

- Bingo (always a big hit!)
- Pictionary (second to Bingo in popularity)
- Games such as checkers, Uno, Othello, Jenga, and board games
- Spectator sports such as baseball, basketball (mostly adults)
- Birthday parties - planning, shopping, and setting up
- Crafts, cutting, pasting, rubber stamps
- Making and sending cards to one another or someone else
- Seasonal crafts such as making ornaments at holiday time
- Roasting marshmallows (at a campfire or at a fireplace!)
- Group singing (have the words written down)
- Making a video of the group and then watching it
- Miniature golf
- Bowling
- Roller skating
- Swinging in a park
- Dances with a D.J.
- Kite-flying
- Swim party
- Costume parties
- Cooking and baking
- Interviewing each other
- Tell-a-joke time
- Talent shows (Remember to videotape!)

Whatever the focus and make-up of the group, consider the following to accommodate the need for familiarity and allow for greater relaxation and fun. Follow these general guidelines:

1. Meet on a consistent basis throughout the year.
2. Keep the group small, or divide a larger group into smaller units.
3. Begin the group meetings with a familiar routine.
4. Display the schedule of events, and provide individual schedules when needed.
5. Provide structure and visual cues.
6. Write social stories to clarify problematic situations, *and to acknowledge positive behavior.*
7. Have a snack or a meal.
8. Discuss and/or vote on what the group will do next time.
9. Conclude with a familiar routine activity.

Drawing by Thomas Johnson, 1996
"The Ruby Slippers"

Chapter 11: Feeling Upset
Workbook

Drawing by Maria White, 1999
–Age 21

Emotions

People feel **emotions** inside of them. *My* emotions are feelings that I have *inside of me*. Some words to describe emotions are *happy, sad, angry, frustrated, scared, worried, anxious, and* _____ .

Most children automatically show how they are feeling through their facial expressions. For example, when a child is happy, a smile will form on his face and he might laugh. When a child is scared, his face will change in a different way. His eyes might open wide and there might be lines on his forehead between his eyes.

It is different for many children with autism.

- My face **might not show** how I feel inside.
- Some people think I do not have emotions because they might not see them on my face.
- My face might show a **different emotion** than what I feel.

For example, a child with autism might be feeling happy, but his face might not show a smile. People might think that he is sad or bored, but he is really happy.

Even if my face doesn't always show it, I feel emotions. My face might not always communicate the feelings that I have inside.

Naming Feelings

Feelings are how people experience emotions. There are **words** that are **names** for different feelings and emotions. Some names for feelings or emotions, are:

Happy	Delighted
Overjoyed	Sad
Angry	Worried
Scared	Depressed
Anxious	Frustrated

As they grow up, most children learn the words that describe how they are feeling inside.

Children with autism have feelings just like everybody, but they might not be able to explain how they are feeling. They might have difficulty finding the words for how they feel. Some children don't know how to identify their feelings. Some children with autism don't know which words match how they feel. Many children with autism don't know that it is possible to communicate how they feel in words.

Answering questions like, *"How do you feel about this?"* can be puzzling for children with autism.

Feeling Anxious

Everyone feels anxious sometimes. **Anxious** means that a person feels worried and confused. He might cry or his hands might tremble, or he might get a stomachache or a headache. Sometimes he feels like running away or hiding. Sometimes feeling anxious makes people feel angry and they might want to scream and yell. Others might get very, very, quiet when they are anxious.

Children with autism seem to get anxious more often than other people. **I will mark what is true for me.** 🖉

I feel anxious when:

► There is too much happening at the same time.

► Something is just not the way it's supposed to be.

► I don't want to do something different.

► There is too much noise or bright light.

► I feel sick.

► I don't understand something.

► Someone is talking too much.

► There are too many people around; I need to be alone.

► I don't know what to do.

► I can't find the words to say.

► I make a mistake.

► I want to be alone.

► other: _____

What Happens When I Feel Anxious

When I feel anxious, my body does certain things automatically. **I will mark what happens to me when I am anxious.** 🖋

- ▶ Stomachache
- ▶ Headache
- ▶ Hands tremble or shake
- ▶ Ringing or buzzing in my ears
- ▶ Just don't feel right
- ▶ Twitching that I don't do on purpose (motor tics)
- ▶ Saying words or sounds, not on purpose (vocal tics)
- ▶ Other: _____

Sometimes children who feel anxious might do some of these things. **I will mark the things that I do.** 🖋

- ▶ Tantrum, yell, or scream
- ▶ Throw something or break something
- ▶ Say *"I don't want to"*
- ▶ Hit, bite, pinch, or scratch someone
- ▶ Run away and hide
- ▶ Get very, very, quiet
- ▶ Bite my hand or hit my head
- ▶ Scratch my arms or face
- ▶ Pick at scabs until they bleed
- ▶ Rock back and forth or move my body in other ways
- ▶ Find someone to talk to
- ▶ Other: _____

Feeling Upset

Being Oppositional

Oppositional means that someone refuses to do what their parent or teacher or someone else wants them to do. It is called *oppositional* because they do or say the *opposite* of what someone wants them to do or say.

Children who are like this often, are described as **being oppositional.**

Many children with autism are not oppositional, but some children with autism can be *very* oppositional.

Some children become oppositional when they are anxious or upset. Sometimes it becomes a habit.

I will (circle) or highlight what is true for me. ✏

> ▶ I can be oppositional, a lot. Often, **I want to do things differently** than what my parent or teacher says.
>
> ▶ I am usually not oppositional. People say that I am "easy-going". Usually, **I do what I am supposed to do.**
>
> ▶ Sometimes I am oppositional, but sometimes I like to do what my parent or teacher says.
>
> ▶ I get oppositional when I am **anxious** or **upset.**
>
> ▶ Being oppositional gets people to leave me alone.
>
> ▶ other: _____

When children are oppositional, it is difficult for other adults and children to play with them. **Other people feel angry when a child is oppositional.** They usually *do not like* to be with a child who is acting oppositional.

Hurting Myself

Once in a while some children with autism try to **hurt themselves.** Parents and teachers and other people feel very worried when children hurt themselves. It is not good for a child to hurt himself. *Some children with autism might try to hurt themselves when they are feeling scared, angry, worried, frustrated, anxious, sad, or confused.*

If I never try to hurt myself, then I do not have to read more on this page. I can turn to the next page. ➔

I will ⟨circle⟩ or highlight what is true for me. ✏

Sometimes I try to hurt myself when:

- ▶ There is too much noise or too much happening.
- ▶ I am not sure what is going to happen.
- ▶ I am overwhelmed.
- ▶ People keep talking to me.
- ▶ I want to be left alone.
- ▶ I am frustrated or angry or worried.
- ▶ I want to say something, but I'm not able to say it.
- ▶ I don't know or understand what to do.
- ▶ Something already hurts. When I hurt myself *more*, it changes or dulls the pain.
- ▶ other: _____

Feeling Upset

Hurting Other People

Once in a while, some children with autism might hit, kick, or scratch people. They might throw things. This is called **aggression** or **being aggressive**. Parents and teachers are very worried when children are aggressive. *It is not good to hurt people or break things.* Usually, most children with autism do not want to hurt anyone on purpose. They probably don't understand how it feels to someone else. But sometimes a child with autism might be very upset or angry, and he might hurt someone who is nearby.

I will (circle) or highlight what is true for me. 🖉

> ▶ I never try to hurt, hit, kick, scratch, or pinch other people.
>
> ▶ Sometimes I have hurt other people.

If I become aggressive and hurt someone, it might be because:

> ▶ I am anxious, scared, frustrated or angry.
>
> ▶ Someone is standing near me when I am upset.
>
> ▶ I am confused and I can't think of what to do.
>
> ▶ I want to get away, but can't. I feel trapped.
>
> ▶ I am so upset that I can't communicate.
>
> ▶ I am angry at my parent or someone else.
>
> ▶ I am angry about _____ .
>
> ▶ other: _____ .

Feeling Upset

Reading Other People's Emotions

Children and adults express emotions in many ways.

- Some people are very expressive. They laugh and cry and yell.

- Some people are quiet with their emotions. They might talk quietly even if they have a lot of feelings. They don't express how they are feeling.

- Most people do some of both.

Many children with autism find it difficult to understand all the different ways that people express their emotions. Children with autism might not know if another person is happy or sad or angry or worried. Or, they might think that the person is very angry, when that person might be feeling something different. They might get the wrong message.

On the next page is an *emotion-meter*. It might help me "read" other people's emotions. It might help me learn to name feelings and emotions. It is like a thermometer that shows different temperatures.

My parent or teacher can make copies of the *emotion-meter*. They can fill it in to show me how they are feeling about something.

Feeling Upset

Emotion-Meter for My Parent

To the parent or teacher or other significant adult,

This is for *you* to fill out *about yourself,* to communicate to your child more accurately **what you are feeling** about an incident or situation. Fill in the information to describe what you are feeling. In the bottom box, indicate the level or degree that most accurately describes the intensity of your emotion in this particular situation. Color it in like a thermometer. Show it to your child to help him accurately "read" how and what you are feeling about the situation. For more ideas, see the section at the end of this chapter *For Parents and Teachers.*

Person's Name (*name of parent, teacher, or other person*)

The situation (*with whom, about what, where, and when*)

The emotion (*Circle the word or write on the lines.*)

Happy Sad Worried Angry Scared Frustrated

or _____ and _____

The Emotion-meter reading (*Color the bar like a thermometer to indicate the appropriate level.*)

The Biggest, Most Intense Feeling ⎯ 3

In the middle, some feeling, but not too much ⎯ 2

Just a tiny bit of feeling ⎯ 1

Emotion-meter for Me

I will mark what is true for me. ✏️

1. Describe the **situation** and the **emotion**, in boxes below.

The situation *(where, when, with whom?)*

The emotion *(Circle words that describe my feeling, or write on the lines.)*

Happy   Sad   Worried   Angry   Scared   Frustrated

or _____   and _____

2. **The Emotion-meter**   *(Color the bar to the level of my feeling.)*

The Biggest, Most Intense Feeling

In the middle, some feeling, but not too much

Just a tiny bit of feeling

3. **What I can do when I am feeling _____:**

Feeling Better

It is not good for a child to hurt himself or others. *Most children with autism will be calmer and happier, and they will not try to hurt themselves or others when they:*

- ☑ Know what is going to happen and when it will be finished.
- ☑ Are familiar with *what* is happening.
- ☑ Are comfortable in the sensory environment; sounds, sights, etc.
- ☑ Exercise every day: walk fast, run, swim, jump, ride a bike, etc.
- ☑ Have time to enjoy their talents and special interests.
- ☑ Learn how to communicate what they need and want.
- ☑ Play with other children in ways that are truly fun for them.
- ☑ Can have frequent "breaks".
- ☑ When things make sense.

I feel calm and happy when _____ .

My parent and teacher can do things to help me feel good. They can try the ideas in this book. This list is for them. They can try:

- ☐ Adding structure (schedules, work systems, lists, etc.)
- ☐ Reducing the sensory stimulation.
- ☐ Helping me exercise every day.
- ☐ Teaching me ways to communicate *easily.*
- ☐ Providing opportunities for my special interests.
- ☐ Giving me frequent breaks and quiet times.
- ☐ Change their expectations for me, socially. Allow social situations to be adapted for me as I grow and learn.
- ☐ Help me become familiar with new things, *gradually.*

Exercise

Exercise keeps my body strong and helps me stay healthy. Exercise that makes my heart beat fast for about 20-30 minutes, once or twice each day, can help me stay calm.

I will (circle) or highlight what is true for me. ✎

I would like to do this kind of exercise:

- ▶ Walking fast
- ▶ Running or jogging
- ▶ Running up a hill and rolling down
- ▶ Jumping on the trampoline
- ▶ Aerobics to music
- ▶ Swimming
- ▶ Dancing to music
- ▶ Riding a bicycle or a stationary bicycle
- ▶ Jumping rope
- ▶ Jumping on a pogo stick
- ▶ Roller skating or in-line skating
- ▶ *If there is snow:* walking up a hill and sledding down.
- ▶ *If there is snow:* snow-shoeing or cross-country skiing.
- ▶ Horseback riding.
- ▶ other: _____
- ▶ other: _____

My schedule shows me when it is time to exercise.

Relaxation

Relaxation means that my body and my mind are feeling calm. I can learn how to relax and stay calm.

With the help of my parent, teacher, or therapist, I can find out what helps me relax.

We can mark some things to try. 🖉

- ▶ Go to my quiet area.
- ▶ Go somewhere else to be alone.
- ▶ Listen to calming music.
- ▶ Listen to my favorite music.
- ▶ Practice slow, deep breathing.
- ▶ Practice a tensing/relaxing muscle routine.
- ▶ Listen to a cassette tape of music and guided visualizations.
- ▶ Watch a video with calming scenes and sounds.
- ▶ Watch a video with a relaxation routine.
- ▶ Think or read about favorite things.
- ▶ Practice slow stretching exercises.
- ▶ Get a massage.
- ▶ *Give* someone a massage.
- ▶ Swing (in the basement, backyard, or in a park).
- ▶ other: _____
- ▶ other: _____

My schedule shows me when it is time to practice relaxation.

Good Nutrition

When people are healthy, they usually *feel better*. They are more able to handle stress and anxiety when their bodies are healthy.

Good nutrition means eating foods that contain a variety of vitamins and minerals, and can help people stay healthy. Healthy people feel better.

- But children with autism might be picky eaters. They might want to only eat certain foods and refuse to try other foods. It might be more difficult for children with autism to get good nutrition.

- Another way to help get good nutrition is by getting vitamins and minerals that are in pills. They are called *vitamins and minerals*, or *nutritional supplements*.

- If I am a very picky eater, then I might get better nutrition by taking vitamins, or nutritional supplements.

My schedule shows me when it is time to take vitamins or supplements.

Counseling

Counseling is when a person goes to an office to talk with a *counselor* or a *therapist*. Sometimes talking with a therapist can help a child learn more about themselves and what to do to feel less anxious. Every child with autism does not talk with a therapist, but some do. Some children who don't have autism go to a therapist, too.

I will (circle) or highlight what is true for me. 🖉

▶ Sometimes I talk with a counselor or a therapist. My therapist's name is _____ .

▶ I do not talk with a counselor or a therapist.

▶ I want to talk with a counselor or a therapist.

▶ My parent says that I might go to a counselor or therapist sometime in the future.

I might do some of these things with a counselor or therapist:

- Write lists
- Mind map
- Draw pictures
- Write stories
- Play game
- Talk and write on the computer
- Read stories
- Draw cartoons
- Role play
- Watch or make videotapes
- Read this book together
- Just talk

Feeling Upset

For Parents and Teachers

"Stress alters everything for me, including sensory stuff, my ability to think, to function, to analyze things.... There can be so much happening beneath the surface that a single event which seems from the outside like one little thing, no big deal, is a trigger for losing everything...."

–Dave Spicer on stress, anxiety, and falling apart

Ideas in This Chapter

✓ Prevention

✓ Self-acceptance

✓ During an outburst

✓ After the outburst

✓ Mind the Gap

✓ Using the emotion-meters

✓ Reevaluate and reassess

✓ Reduce sensory stimulation

✓ Exercise

✓ Frequent breaks

✓ The quiet area

✓ Relaxation

✓ Diet and nutrition

✓ Counseling

✓ Medication

✓ Tics

✓ A special note about adolescence

Prevention

Visually structured teaching, especially when the strategies are adapted for an individual child, can dramatically affect behavior in a positive way. Uncertainty leads to anxiety, which leads to behavior problems. Reread the ideas in previous chapters and implement the suggestions that meet your child's needs. Adapt, modify, and individualize the strategies until they fit. *Provide meaning for your child in ways that he can see and understand. The more that things make sense to your child, the less anxious he will be.*

Children with autism are less likely to tantrum or become upset when:

1. They know what is going to happen and when it will be finished.
2. People, activities, and things in the environment are familiar.
3. Sensory stimulation in the environment is reduced.
4. They engage in regular physical activity, daily.
5. They can enjoy their strengths, talents, and special interests.
6. They learn to communicate their needs and wants, effectively.
7. Social situations fit their desires and abilities.
8. They have frequent "breaks".
9. Their daily activities are meaningful to them.

Most of the strategies that have been introduced in previous chapters remain relevant and necessary as preventative behavior management strategies. Review previous chapters and implement the strategies that are indicated for your child.

Self-acceptance

Your child's anxiety may lessen as he gains better understanding of himself. Make this book, especially the personally meaningful pages, available to him often. When appropriate for your child, talk and/or write about having autism and other related personal issues. Emphasize the positive qualities and acknowledge the challenges. Help him see that he is not alone and that there are other people, with and without autism, who experience the same things.

During an outburst

In the midst of your child's outburst, remember to inhibit your natural inclination to talk, explain, or otherwise verbally process what is happening. In other words, *don't talk!* Usually, the most important things you can do *during* a behavioral crisis are (1) keep your child safe from self-injury, (2) keep others safe from injury, and (3) be quiet.

This means that if your child is not self-injurious or aggressive, probably the most important single thing you can do at the time of the outburst is to be quiet. Of course, there may be individual children for whom a specific verbal routine is calming; however, in most cases, it is best not to add to the confusion and extreme anxiety by talking.

If something must be communicated during an outburst, you can write it down. Keep the message simple and clear. Quietly hand the written note to your child, or place it somewhere where he will see it. If it is more convenient and your child can see it easily, you may even want to post the note on to a wall, a door, or on a nearby piece of furniture. If your child is lying on the floor, you can place the note next to him, close to his face, so he can see it. In some cases, hold the note up in front of his eyes so he can read it. Do not say anything while you are doing this, and try not to make eye contact.

If your child's outburst is loud and disruptive to others, he needs to go to a more private space during the disruption, if possible. You can remind him of this with a *written note*. **Remember, usually it is better if you do not try to talk to him at this time.**

After the outburst

After your child recovers from the outburst, and has calmed down, you may want to communicate about what happened. Do this verbally *and* visually. (Talk *and* write.) Reread the workbook chapters and the ideas in Chapter 6 about *understanding*. Use a strategy that you both are comfortable with and that meets your child's needs. *This is when your consistent use of these strategies on a daily basis really pays off.*

The more familiar your child is with using visual strategies, the easier it will be for him to communicate and learn, and the easier it will be for both of you to prevent, and handle, being upset.

Try writing notes by hand, using a computer to write and talk, drawing pictures and diagrams, Comic Strip Conversations, social stories, and/or clarifying with a schedule or list. Reading the relevant workbook pages in this book, together with your child, may help you and your child identify the issue and decide on a preventative plan for the future. A strategy that may work for your child is called *Mind the gap.*

Mind the Gap

Many children with autism or Asperger Syndrome are surprised and confused at their *own* reactions to stress and anxiety. It may seem to your child, that his emotional response has come out of the blue–unexpectedly–and suddenly he is in the midst of a meltdown and out of control. *Mind the gap* is a strategy that has been used to help children and teenagers learn to be aware of their internal state, to give them control over their response to an event, and to teach positive behavior. Readers from London will be familiar with this term; it is the recorded message that is heard upon disembarking the *tube* (subway). The announcement "Mind the gap!" reminds travelers to be careful of the gap between the train and the platform. The American equivalent is "Watch your step!"

Several years ago, Jack Wall, the director of the Charlotte TEACCH Center, decided that this concept could be used to describe the period between anxiety-building incidents, and the individual's reaction. Jack, traveling in England at the time, found himself thinking about a particular child's outbursts when he noticed t-shirts with the phrase "Mind the Gap!" being sold in the subway station. This strategy resulted.

Borrowing the phrase, "Mind the Gap!" the emphasis is placed on helping the child become aware of the "zone" or the "gap" at which time a choice can be made as to what actions to take. Teresa Johnson, a Parent Advocate for the Autism Society of North Carolina (and mother of Thomas, one of this book's illustrators), promotes its use with parents and teachers of high functioning children and teenagers. Some children have become more aware of the build-up of anxiety within, the external events which may be at their cause, and finally, what to do about it. Teresa emphasizes that all children are different; in order for your child to be successful, adaptations must be made in how you develop and use *Mind the Gap.* You may want to change the name to something more meaningful to your child. For one teenager, it was called the *Decision Zone.* It can be used in coordination with behavior management point systems, or it can be used simply as a visual reminder about the process of stress build-up, and what to do to avoid negative consequences. Social stories can be written to show how *Mind the Gap* fits into daily life. On the next page is a sample, followed by the general guidelines to help you individualize this strategy for your child.

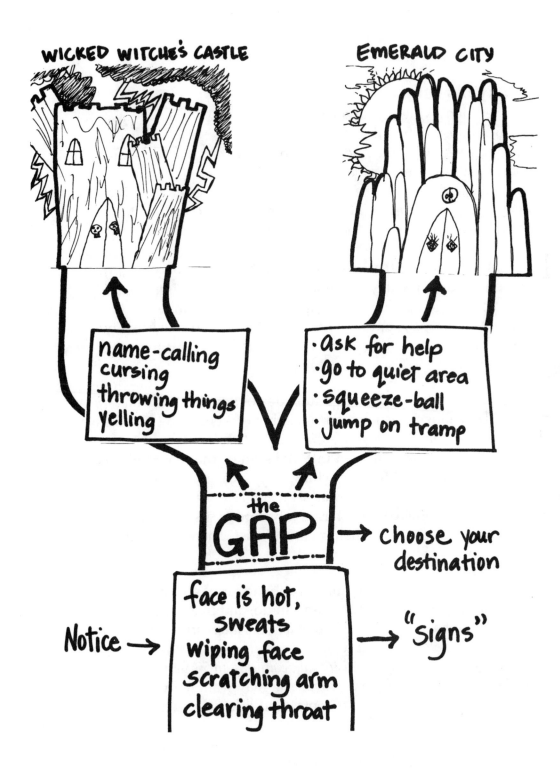

WICKED WITCHE'S CASTLE

EMERALD CITY

name-calling
cursing
throwing things
yelling

· ask for help
· go to quiet area
· squeeze-ball
· jump on tramp

the
GAP → choose your
destination

Notice → face is hot,
sweats
wiping face
scratching arm
clearing throat

→ "signs"

1. Identify the behaviors to target

First, before sitting down with the child, the adult must prepare by identifying which behaviors to target. *Examples are: name-calling, cursing, self-injury, or throwing things.*

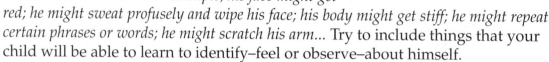

2. Identify his "signs"

After identifying the targeted behaviors, make a mental list, noting the observable "signs" that the child exhibits sometime before the behavioral outburst. *For example, his face might get red; he might sweat profusely and wipe his face; his body might get stiff; he might repeat certain phrases or words; he might scratch his arm...* Try to include things that your child will be able to learn to identify–feel or observe–about himself.

3. Sit down with your child and make three lists

Now, sit down with your child at a time when he is calm, and explain that together, you are going to make a map that will help him feel better and make good choices when he is upset. **Write the list of the targeted behaviors** on a piece of paper or a large index card. Introduce this list in a matter-of-fact, calm manner.

Next, introduce your child to the idea of how his body has specific sensations or feelings, or shows certain behaviors before he gets outwardly upset. *You can use pages from the workbook–Chapter 11–to help with this.* **Make a list with your child of the observable and internal signals that your child can feel and see.** This may be difficult for your child, so you can say something like, *"I noticed that before you yelled yesterday, you had scratched your arm and it became very red."* The list can be written by hand or on the computer, using fonts and styles of your child's design. Your child can help make this list if he wants, but it is not necessary.

Now make a list of the (positive) behavioral alternatives. Come up with a few simple strategies that your child can do, and that can be used effectively in different situations. Be specific. *For example, list alternative words to say (instead of cursing); how to ask for help; how to take a break (how to leave and where to go); and other practices like squeezing a squishy ball; counting to 50; deep breathing; going to a special place to punch or beat a bean-bag...* You may want to brainstorm ideas ahead of time with other teachers and parents. And don't forget to ask your child for ideas, also!

4. Draw a map with two destinations

Draw a "map" with your child, using a high interest theme or topic. In the diagram the previous page, the adult drew the roads and Thomas drew the two destinations on the top, at the end of the roads. Thomas has chose *The Emerald City* to represent the positive outcomes, and *The Wicked Witch's Castle* to represent the undesireable outcomes. Attach the three lists at the appropriate places on the map, as shown in the diagram.

It is important that your child participate in creating the pictures of the two destinations. If he likes to draw, supply him with paper and pens. If he is not an artist, then he can find pictures from magazines to represent his positive and negative images. He can use photographs or postcards. Recently, a child used Pokemon cards for the two locations: a "good Pokemon" and a "bad Pokemon". Encourage your child to use what is most meaningful to him.

Connect the "good behavior" with the positive outcome. For some children, points are earned or taken away. For others, the visual image of the positive and negative destinations are powerful enough. Special treats, videos, time on Nintendo, a trip to the art suppy store, or other personally motivating activities may be effective.

5. Things to keep in mind

Keys to this strategy seem to be that it is visual, and that it is personally meaningful to the child in a concrete way. Teresa emphasizes that it must be interactive; refer to it, and change and adapt the lists as the child changes. Try to help him identify his body's reaction to stress, keeping in mind that he might not be able to recognize it, yet. Until he learns his body's "signals", you can help him by calmly pointing them out, when they occur. *"You are scratching your arm,"* and then point to the *Mind the gap* picture, drawing his attention to the lists and the behaviors that lead to the different destinations. You can literally point out (without talking) the positive behavioral alternatives which will propel him down the road to his positive destination.

Posters can be made and displayed in different locations (different rooms of the house and different locations at school). Teresa suggests that parents make small, index-card size copies to post in the car and carry in a purse or pocket, so the visual cue is always available. She discovered that after Thomas became used to *seeing* the posters, she just had to remind him (when he was approaching the "gap") about making a choice between *"The Emerald City or The Witch's Castle."*

Using the emotion-meters

Many children have trouble "reading" how their parent or teacher feels. Some children assume that the adult is quite angry, when it may not really be the case, or vice versa. Children with autism often have difficulty detecting the subtle differences in types of emotions or degrees of emotion. Some children may overreact simply because they misinterpret the adult's reaction. If this causes problems for you and your child, you might try experimenting with the **Emotion-meter for My Parent** (page 252) to clarify how *you* are feeling.

Duplicate the workbook page and keep extras on hand, so it is always available. First, practice using the emotion-meter to illustrate your feelings when no one is upset. Remember to use it to illustrate happy feelings, as well as troubled ones. The more frequently you use it in daily life, the more familiar it will become. *As with all visually structured strategies, once it is a familiar routine to your child, it will become more powerful and effective during a crisis.*

You can also try teaching him to use an emotion-meter, to describe his *own* emotions *(page 253). The emotion-meter might become a tool to help your child notice, identify, and communicate his internal emotional state. He might also begin to understand that there are different degrees of feelings, and how to be aware of these internal feelings.* On page 253, there is an **Emotion-meter for Me**. Teach your child how to fill it in. At the bottom of page 253, there is a space on which to write a positive behavioral course of action. Depending on your child, possibilities could be going to the quiet area, jumping on the trampoline, writing a letter on the computer, or other activities.

Reevaluate and reassess

If tantrums, aggression, or self-injurious behavior persist on a regular basis, even though you have added more structure to your child's life, you will need to step back, reevaluate, and reassess. Further simplify and increase the visually structured strategies, and make sure that he is getting regular physical

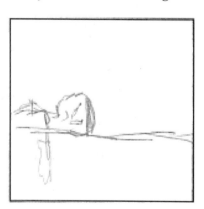

activity. Look more closely at sensory issues, and make accommodations in the environment. Try to see your child's daily life through his eyes and imagine it through his senses. Review the list under the previous heading, **Prevention,** page 260. *What might be causing anxiety? What needs to be modified? Does he need to communicate something more effectively?* Add more structure, exercise, use his special interests, give him breaks, try social stories, and simplify demands.

For additional in-depth information on understanding and developing strategies to handle and prevent your child's angry outbursts, see the book **Asperger Syndrome and Difficult Moments**, by Myles and Southwick. (It may also be found under its original title, **Asperger Syndrome and Rage**, by the same authors.) Several assessment instruments and suggestions for developing management plans for school and home are included in this book listed in the *Recommended Resources*.

Reduce sensory stimulation

Respect the sensory differences that accompany autism. Review Chapter 3 and your child's personal responses of his sensory experiences. Adapt where possible and when indicated. Incorporate regular physical activity and frequent breaks in his daily schedule.

Exercise

Develop an exercise program for your child and include it in his daily schedule. Running and other physical activity helps reduce the build-up of anxiety, and often results in a marked decrease in self-injurious and aggressive behavior. For some children, two exercise periods each day may be helpful. *See the workbook page 254 for exercise ideas, and page 45 for an example of exercise time included on a child's schedule.*

Frequent breaks

Allow your child to take frequent breaks. Show him on his schedule when it the breaks will happen. Include a break time for his favorite activity on his work system for **"what will happen next?"**. Give him breaks to go to the quiet area. Give him breaks after new or unfamiliar activities, and before and after dealing with new or unfamiliar people. Give him breaks after unexpected events and surprises. Frequent breaks will help him recover from possible confusion and overstimulation; regain an inner calm; pace himself for the day's demands; prevent the build-up of anxiety; and summon the much-needed energy and stamina with which to handle the world and its surprises. *For information on schedules and work systems, see pages 36-49, 167, 171-173, 191-192, and 194-196.*

The quiet area

The quiet area is a place of respite; a "get-away" for your child. He probably already has something like this, on his own...his own retreat. By creating an "official" quiet area, you are acknowledging his need to have time to be alone and get calm and centered. You are also structuring a way to teach him an important adaptive skill that he can use to prevent the build-up of anxiety. The quiet area has been mentioned and discussed in previous chapters. *See pages 64, 186, and 211 for more information about the quiet area.*

Relaxation

Teach relaxation routines and visual imagery through the use of written or picture directions. Try tape-recorded instructions, music, and video-tapes. You might want to find a therapist who is experienced with these types of strategies to help you locate resources.

Like with other strategies, it is important to build a positive, preventative routine by having your child learn and practice "relaxation" on a regular, daily basis. Do not wait until he is upset before you introduce the music, picture cues, video, or guided routine. *The more familiar he is with a certain strategy, the more effective it will be when you want him to use it in times of real need. See page 255 for specific ideas, and page 45 for an example of relaxation time included in a schedule.*

Diet and nutrition

There is an abundance of nutritional advice available in bookstores, natural food stores, and on the Internet. Many children with autism have very rigid food preferences. The combination of these two factors can make "diet and nutrition" a very confusing subject for parents of children with autism.

Some dietary regimes are said to have dramatic effects for children with autism. Often, high costs are involved, as well as a change of lifestyle and food restrictions. Choosing a special diet is a personal decision on the part of the family of the child with autism and their health care practitioner. Especially when contemplating expensive, time-consuming, and dramatic changes in diet, it is advisable to become as educated as possible about the diet.

Look for research and talk with other parents who have tried the diet with their child. Consult with your doctor. *What are the pros and cons? Is this something you will be able to follow through with every day? Will your child cooperate?* If you decide to try a particular diet with your child, use his schedule and other visual strategies to prepare him for the changes in his meal routines and food choices. Be sure to allow a realistic trial period, after which you can evaluate the diet's effectiveness.

Most of us realize that the health of our bodies is directly affected by the type and quality of the food we ingest, along with other lifestyle factors. It is common sense that the better we feel, the better we are able to handle the demands and stresses of daily life. This is true for your child, as well. It is important to help him eat in a healthy manner, as much as possible. This may be extremely difficult if your child is a picky eater. There may be particular vitamins or supplements that will support his overall health. *(See p. 46 for an example of a schedule indicating a time to take vitamins.)* It is comforting to know that most parents of older children and adults with autism will say that as their children grew up, they were more willing to try new food and became less rigid about food. If you have questions or concerns about your child's nutrition, you should consult a knowledgable physician or nutritionist, especially those who are familiar with a variety of children with autism.

Counseling

Some children with high functioning autism and Asperger Syndrome may benefit from counseling, but therapies which require examining one's feelings and emotional processing are often not very effective with most children with

autism. Find a therapist who is familiar with *(or who wants to learn about)* high functioning autism and Asperger Syndrome, and the particular ways in which children with autism think and learn. Call your local chapter of the Autism Society for referrals. Many of the ideas in this book, as well as the workbook itself, could be a useful tool during counseling sessions.

Medication

If severe aggression and self-injurious behavior continue, you may want to talk with your physician about medication that might decrease anxiety and other related symptoms. If your physician is not experienced with the types of medications currently used with children who have autism, ask for a referral to a psychiatrist who is familiar with treating children with autism.

Tics

If your child has frequent vocal or motor tics (involuntary sounds, words, or movements) that are increasing or that are causing problems, you may want to talk with a psychiatrist who is familiar with both autism and Tourette Syndrome. Some children with autism or Asperger Syndrome may also be affected by Tourette Syndrome (TS). Symptoms of TS can be triggered by anxiety. For more information about TS, visit the Tourette Syndrome Association Web site at www.tsa.mgh.harvard.edu.

A special note about adolescence

Your child may be entering adolescence or may already be there. Although this book was written with younger people in mind, many adolescents with autism may benefit from the workbook. The ideas in the sections for parents and teachers remain valid for most individuals with autism of any age, as well.

Gary Mesibov, the director of Division TEACCH at the University of North Carolina at Chapel Hill, reminds us that just like any child reaching adolescence, the child with autism has some very specific and basic needs. They are:

The need for privacy—time to himself.

The need to be more independent—to make more choices for himself.

It is not surprising that if these basic needs are not met, your older child may become anxious or angry, and behavior problems may result. The same thing happens for any adolescent, whether he has autism or not. Remember and plan for these needs as your child grows.

Older children with autism often still require help with basic needs; hair washing, bathing, teethbrushing, choosing clothing, and other self-care skills. Problems with sequencing, sensory confusion, and being dependent on prompts, often result in parents having to do more than they or the child really want. It is frustrating for all involved.

If you and the teachers have already taught your child how to follow schedules, work systems, and check lists, you are a step ahead of the game! You have built in a way to help your child be more independent as he grows, while still providing the guidance and support that is necessary. Options and choices can be structured into the schedule. Providing checklists for chores, assignments, and especially self-care skills, will help you give him the privacy he needs and the independence he craves.

Chapter 12: The Last Chapter

Workbook

Drawing by Maria White, 1999, age 21

Statistics About Autism

- For every 1,000 people in the world, there are approximately 2 people who have autism. That is a ratio of about 2 per 1,000.

- For every 5 people with autism, 4 of them are male and 1 is female. That is a ratio of 4 boys to 1 girl.

- There are children and adults with autism living in every country in the world.

- There are children and adults with autism in every state of the United States.

- In North Carolina, where this book was written, there are approximately 14,000 people* who have autism. To estimate the number of people with autism in your state or country, follow the directions on the next page. →

---

*1999 estimate from the *Spectrum*, the newsletter of the *Autism Society of North Carolina (ASNC)*.

Statistics Worksheet

I live in the state (or country) of _____.

The population of my state (or country) is _____.
If I don't know the population, I can look it up on the
Internet or in an encyclopedia.

I can follow these instructions to estimate the number of
people with autism in my state or country. **I will ask
someone to help me.** ✏

1. Write the population number in Box 1.

2. Divide by 1,000.

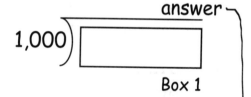

3. Write the answer in Box 2.

4. Multiply by 2.

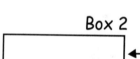

5. Circle your answer.

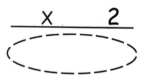

6. Write the circled answer on the first line in the
   sentence below.

There are approximately _____ people with autism
in _____ (state or country), where I live.

Being Unique

No one is exactly the same. Everyone is different and special. This means that everyone is *unique*.

- Every child looks and sounds unique.
- Every child has unique thoughts, hopes and fears.
- Every child has unique strengths and talents.
- It is OK to be different. Everyone is unique.

Many children try to look and act and talk like each other. This is called "fitting in". Many children try to "fit in" instead of feeling comfortable *being unique*.

Children with autism often find it difficult to "fit in". Some children with autism do not care if they "fit in". Some children with autism try to "fit in", but they may not know what to do.

Trying to "fit in" is not fun for most children with autism.

**It is OK to not fit in.
I am unique.
It is perfectly OK to be me.**

*More on **being unique...***

Here are few examples of the ways everyone is unique:

- hair, skin, and eye color
- height and weight
- styles of clothing
- kinds of homes
- sound of voice
- language we speak
- strengths and talents
- things we like
- style of learning

I will (circle) or highlight what is true for me. ✏

▶ The color of my hair is different from the color of my parent's hair.

▶ The color of my (name of relative)_____ 's eyes are different from the color of my eyes.

▶ The clothes that my friend wears are different from the clothes that I wear.

▶ My house is different from my neighbor's house.

▶ My teacher's voice is different from my parent's voice.

▶ The language I speak is different from the language that the children who live in Italy speak.

▶ I am good at_____ .
Another child, whose name is _____ , is good at _____ .

▶ I like to learn about (subject) _____ . A different child I know, whose name is_____ , likes to learn about (subject) _____ .

What is Respect?

Respect describes how all people should treat one another. Respect is like a *circle* with *two halves*.

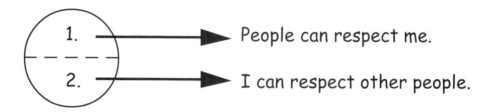

    1. **People can respect me.** When people try to understand me, they respect me. When people know that autism is not wrong, but that it is just a different way of being, they respect me. When people know that I am a whole person with strengths and weaknesses, likes and dislikes, dreams and fears, they respect me. When they like me just the way I am, they respect me. *Reading this book might help people understand and respect me.*

2. **I can respect other people.** I can try to remember that each person has his or her own thoughts. Each person has unique strengths, likes, dreams, and fears. Even if I don't understand why they are that way, I can respect other people. *When someone is different from me, it does not mean that he or she is wrong.*

I show respect when I try to be polite and not make fun of, or say bad things about my brothers, sisters, friends, teachers, parents, and other children or adults.

All people deserve respect.

The Last Chapter

How All Children Are the Same

All children want others to understand and respect them. All children are unique individuals. All children deserve respect.

This is how all children are the same. ⬆

I will (circle) or highlight what is true for me. ✏

- ▶ I want other people to understand me.
- ▶ I like it when other children understand me.
- ▶ Even if I am different from someone else, I am OK.
- ▶ I want other children to know that having autism is not wrong.
- ▶ I like it when my parent understands me.
- ▶ I like it when my teacher understands me.
- ▶ I try to remember that other children have their own thoughts. Their thoughts might be different from my thoughts. That is OK.
- ▶ Even if someone else is different from me, he or she is OK.
- ▶ I can respect someone else, even if he or she says things that I do not agree with.
- ▶ I want to understand other children better.
- ▶ I want to understand _____ (name) better.
- ▶ I want _____ (name) to understand me.
- ▶ other: _____

Writing a Letter About Me

Dear _____ , (The name of a friend or relative.)

I am writing you a letter to help us understand each other better.

I have autism. Autism affects the way I think and communicate and understand things. Autism is one thing about me. There are other things about me, too.

My favorite things are _____

_____ .

What are your favorite things?

I can do some things very well. I am good at _____

_____ .

What kinds of things are you good at?

Some things are harder for me. I need help with _____

_____ .

What kinds of things do you need help with?

I am glad that we know each other. Please write back to me. Maybe we can learn from each other and have fun getting to know each other.

From,

_____ (my name)

Summary

In small towns, there may be only a few people who have autism. In big cities, there may be hundreds or thousands of people who have autism.

In my school, I may be the only child with autism, or there may be others.

I have some things in common with other children who have autism, although the similarities might be hard to see. Children with autism are different from each other.

- All children are unique.

- Even though all children are unique, they are all the same in one important way. Most children want other people to understand and respect them.

- I want other people to understand and respect me.

- I can learn to respect other people, too.

About the Illustrations

All of the drawings are by people who have autism, except:
Office, p. 169, by Linda Larsen; and *Office with work system*, p. 193, *Organization of work area*, p. 197, and *Folder task example*, p. 199, by Catherine Faherty.

Small sketches in the sections: *For Parents and Teachers*:
The seventy pen-and-pencil sketches that complement the sections *For Parents and Teachers* throughout the book, were drawn by Thomas Johnson, 1999, age 10.

The photographs:
The photographs on pages 285-291 and page 300 are by Marilyn Ferikes, 1999.

The drawings on the title pages of the workbook:

Chapter 1 **Medium:** pen
    Subject: *Pinocchio*
    Artist: Thomas Johnson, 1999, age 10

Chapter 2 **Medium:** pencil
    Subject: *Building a spiraling tower of blocks*, from photo of Doug, by the author at Bell Elementary School in 1986
    Artist: Maria White, 1999, age 21

Chapter 3 **Medium:** pen and pencil
    Subject: *Scarecrow with sun and bird*, and *Feelings*
    Artist: Thomas Johnson, 1992, 1996, at ages 3 and 7

Chapter 4 **Medium:** pencil
    Subject: *Fiddler*, from photo of John Engle, by the author
    Artist: Maria White, 1999, age 21

Chapter 5 **Medium:** pencil, crayon, ink (computer collage by Irene Vassos)
    Subject: *People*
    Artists: Brian Davis, age 14, two views of *Boy with cowlick*
Thomas Johnson, age 5, *My kindergarten teacher*, *Dorothy*, and *Tall woman*
Thomas Johnson, age 10, *Four pencil sketches of people*
Paul Hoyt, age 13, *Three little people*

Chapter 6	**Medium:**	pen on notebook paper
	Subject:	*My first grade teacher*
	Artist:	Thomas Johnson, 1995, age 6

Chapter 7	**Medium:**	pen
	Subject:	*Thinking*, from an old family photograph, early 1900s
	Artist:	Thomas Johnson, 1999, age 10

Chapter 8	**Medium:**	pen on notebook paper
	Subject:	*Dorothy being welcomed to Munchkin Land*
	Artist:	Thomas Johnson, 1995, age 6

Chapter 9	**Medium:**	pencil
	Subject:	*Classroom*, from photograph of author presenting *Understanding Friends* to a fourth-grade class at Bell Elementary School in 1987
	Artist:	Maria White, 1999, age 21

Chapter 10	**Medium:**	pencil
	Subject:	*Friends*, from photograph of the author's students at Bell Elementary School in 1986
	Artist:	Maria White, 1999, age 21

Chapter 11	**Medium:**	pencil
	Subject:	*Autistic girl, after managing her pain by slamming against a wall* (artist's original idea and description)
	Artist:	Maria White, 1999, age 21

Chapter 12	**Medium:**	pencil
	Subject:	*Autistic boy and his olfactory sense* (artist's original idea and description)
	Artist:	Maria White, 1999, age 21

About the Illustrators

Doug Buckner

Take a close look at the Christmas Card design by Doug Buckner, on page 200. Fascinated with houses, buildings, and castles, Doug drew this picture for a Christmas Card contest when he was eleven years old. This particular design wasn't chosen by the judges, however his other entries, more typical and quite charming Christmas scenes, won the contest in 1991 and then again in 1993. They appeared on the *Autism Society of North Carolina Christmas Cards* those two years. But *this one* was always my favorite!

The drawing on page 21, by Maria White is from a photograph I took of Doug when he was five years old, engaged in one of his most favorite free-time activities in the classroom—building. Doug really liked structures. Once, when he was six, Doug built a very familiar looking block structure; it reminded me of something in particular that I knew I had seen before, but I couldn't quite place it. Doug solved the mystery by telling me it was the *Biltmore House*, the famous large castle-like home visited by tourists here in Asheville! Even before Doug began talking, he was drawing houses, houses, and more houses. As time passed, his drawings turned into ornate castles.

Congratulations to Doug on his recent graduation from high school. At the time of this writing, he is involved in the TEACCH Supported Employment program, and is preparing for work in the community. Doug, now 21 years old, is skilled at computer graphics. He is one of the members of the "computer" social group mentioned on page 239. Doug, with his gentle spirit, is also skilled at working with animals.

The first year Doug began school at age five, was the first year I taught a class of young students with autism. We learned a lot together! Six years later, while I was working as a therapist at the TEACCH Center, Doug, eleven years old at the time, was the first child to whom I explained what it meant to "have autism." Thank you Doug, for planting the seed for this book.

Brian Davis

I first saw Brian's drawings when he came to the TEACCH Center for a diagnostic evaluation when he was thirteen. Brian Davis, now fifteen, is fascinated with animation, science fiction movies, and especially drawing comic strips. He is quite passionate about his creations and is into a particular style of drawing that is popular in Japan. A small sample of his artwork (*two boys with cowlicks*) is found in the "People collage" on page 81, and on page 279 of the workbook.

Brian, with his active imagination, has developed an entire culture called "Fantasy Isle" in his comic strips. His main characters, each with their own unique personality, live on an island and have names like *Sparkles, Star, Snowball, Jack, Mike, Flower, Pup,* and the bad guy, *King Wik*. Brian seems to have an uncanny ability to closely observe and represent personality traits with just a few sentences and skilled strokes of the pencil.

Brian's room is filled with boxes and boxes of his drawings. He is beginning to take art classes at school and has recently begun to add a little color to some of his drawings. Brian is in the eighth grade and has been known to sell some of his artwork to admiring classmates.

Paul Hoyt

A sample of the whimsical creations of Paul Hoyt can be found on page 10 *(Three Amigos)*, in the collage on page 81 *(Three little people)*, and on the back cover. Paul has had several one-man art shows featuring his delightfully detailed and colorful drawings. Beginning at an early age, his fascination with Disney characters and related themes eventually made their way to pen and paper. Currently at age 13, Paul voraciously draws very tiny detailed characters, trains, and other perky subjects, which he cuts out and arranges on paper to create captivating miniature scenes. One of Paul's drawings was chosen for the *Autism Society of North Carolina Christmas Card* in 1994.

Despite the fact that no one was sure if Paul was ever going to communicate verbally, he has bloomed in a rich environment of unconditional acceptance, love, and support of his family and the consistent use of visually structured teaching at school and home. Paul now talks once in a while, but he communicates more frequently and spontaneously through the written and typed word, and of course, through his outstanding artwork.

Paul and his family were featured in *Paul at Three*, a film produced by Dave Horn and the *Autism Society of North Carolina*, and WFMY-TV, Raleigh, NC. It was broadcast on North Carolina Public Television in November of 1992. *Paul at Three* is an intimate look into a family with a recently diagnosed three-year old with autism. It very poignantly explores his family's early experience about having a young child with autism and their hopes for his future. The film also introduces the viewers to the TEACCH Program and ASNC (Autism Society of North Carolina). More information about *Paul at Three*, TEACCH, and ASNC, can be found in the *Recommended Resources* at the end of this book.

Thomas Johnson

Adding grace and charm throughout the pages in the sections *For Parents and Teachers* are Thomas' small sketches. He created over seventy drawings for the pages of this book. Earlier drawings from his extensive collection are featured on several of the title pages and scattered throughout the book. Thomas Johnson, an eleven-year-old whose class sampled the workbook, said that this book was *"a very important project for all children with autism"* and that he was *"very happy to help."* Thomas was diagnosed with autism when he was almost four years old.

Thomas' considerable creativity and knowledge has evolved from his first special interest in the *Wizard of Oz* at an early age. The *tornado* sparked his study of weather. The *film* sparked his study of MGM, acting, and producing. *Judy Garland* sparked an interest in Mickey Rooney. *Drawing* the characters and scenes from the story initiated a thorough study of his favorite illustrators: Maurice Sendak and Steven Kellog. Thomas has written and illustrated books for school projects and at home for recreation. While attending summer day camp run by the Western Chapter of the Autism Society of North Carolina, Thomas drew a weekly comic strip *(travel adventures on a magic carpet)* for the newsletter. At the time of this writing, Thomas is enthralled with puppetry. He has spent several hours on Saturdays helping a local puppeteer in her studio, creating puppets and learning all about this art form and the production of puppet shows.

Before beginning the sketches for this book, Thomas assured me that he would represent a wide range of subjects: boys and girls, young and old, and from all racial groups.

Thomas is a fair-minded, kind, and friendly child whose sweet manner touches the heart of all who know him.

Maria White

Maria White very diligently worked on her six beautiful drawings for this book *(pp. 21, 69, 165, 215, 243, and 271)* despite a busy life of working at a video store, taking care of her cats, frequenting her favorite coffee shop, attending her TEACCH Social Groups, and the never-ending chores of everyday life. After seeing her drawing of the boy featured on the title page of Chapter 12 made into a silhouette and repeated throughout the book, Maria remarked, *"I didn't realize that I was creating a new icon for autism!"*

Maria, who is looking for a new job with the help of the TEACCH Supported Employment Program, was diagnosed with autism at age fifteen when she moved to North Carolina. Since then she has been a regular participant on panels of adolescents and adults with autism at our teacher trainings. Maria is committed to helping teachers and the public understand autism. For leisure, Maria enjoys attending art shows, plays, musicals, concerts, and movies. She particularly enjoys listening to music while drawing.

A few years ago, when I was preparing for a trip to Mexico City to give a workshop on autism and structured teaching, Maria, who studied Spanish in high school and had some extra time during that summer vacation, agreed to help by writing a short essay in Spanish about having autism. Maria worked for days until the essay was finished. I videotaped her reading the essay and brought it with me to Mexico, sharing it with the group of over two hundred Mexican teachers, parents, and doctors. Afterwards, I returned to Asheville with my suitcase full of letters, cards, and gifts expressing the audience's awe and gratitude to Maria for sharing her experiences so eloquently.

Here is a picture of Maria *(right)* and the author *(left)*.
I am honored to be Maria's mentor.

About Other Major Contributors

Kelly Davis

Kelly is a busy, creative person. Her enthusiasm for editing the parent and teacher sections of this book comes from both personal and professional experience. Kelly Davis, who by education is a historian, has worked in advertising and publishing for fifteen years. She currently is a book buyer for a distributor based in Asheville, NC. Kelly is a single parent whose two children have high functioning autism. Kelly's assistance and perspective came as a refreshing boost during the completion phase of this book.

Our meetings took place in an unusual office—at a table at a McDonald's Funland. We were able to talk *(quickly)* while her five year old daughter and eight year old son played. Despite her busy life, Kelly spent many hours engaged in this book; reading, rereading, editing, questioning, and making suggestions.

Teresa Johnson

Teresa's encouragement and support was evident during all the phases of this book. Early on, she suggested that her son Thomas contribute the small sketches for the parent and teacher sections. She helped structure his "assignments", kept him on track, and searched through boxes of his drawings, looking for some that I might be able to use. Teresa, a single parent of Thomas and his older sister, Maegan, works for the Autism Society of North Carolina as a Parent Advocate.

In her role as ASNC Parent Advocate, Teresa is committed to strengthening communication between parents, teachers, and school administrators, while keeping her focus on discovering and promoting what is most beneficial for each individual child. She enjoys teaching how to use visual strategies, in particular, schedules and *Mind the Gap*, which was presented in Chapter 11 to help children and teenagers with autism gain a deeper understanding about their individual responses to anxiety, and their power to choose positive behavior with the help of visual teaching strategies. Teresa's dedication to her family and her passion for her work is inspiring.

John Engle

When I write (and talk), I have the tendency to repeat myself. John Engle, who insists on having a clear, orderly, and especially uncluttered environment, did an amazing job of editing the wording in the workbook pages. He located every bit of inconsistency, disagreeing pronouns, unnecessary repetition and redundancy...all of my verbal clutter! However, some pages were written after John returned his edits to me. If there still remain faults such as these, this author takes full responsibility for them. John, who has obsessive-compulsive disorder in addition to high functioning autism, *never* would have let them pass!

You can see Maria's drawing of John playing his fiddle on page 69. John is a gifted musician, artist, and philosopher. His special interests now at thirty-one years of age are old time mountain music and eastern philosophy. John, who does not read music, is accomplished on the banjo and Hawaiian slack-key guitar, in addition to the fiddle. When he was learning the banjo, he figured out forty-seven ways to tune the strings, simply by listening to recordings. He has limited himself to knowing and playing *only seven-hundred* fiddle tunes, because, as he explains, after seven-hundred, *"I start playing tunes I like less, and not playing tunes I like more."* John has built banjos by hand, including a beautiful primitive gourd banjo. One of his essays, along with the original photograph I took of him on the fiddle playing outside of the TEACCH Center, was published in the fall 1997 issue of *The Morning News*, a quarterly publication edited by Carol Gray of Jenison, Michigan.

John, whose diagnosis came when he was twenty-six, has been a regular volunteer at the Asheville TEACCH Center and at the Autism Society of North Carolina's Asheville office. He frequently is on the high functioning autism adolescent and adult panels in our trainings.

I have learned much from John during our long, thought-provoking, conversations. He is quoted many times in this book. John has recently promised to help me with my next big project, learning to play the accordion.

Dave Spicer

Dave is quoted at the beginning of most of the sections for parents and teachers. He also wrote the parent and teacher section at the end of Chapter 4. Dave's diagnosis of high functioning autism/Asperger Syndrome came later in

life, after bringing his son to TEACCH for an evaluation in 1994. Both Dave and his son have a diagnosis of high functioning autism. Since that time, Dave has contributed to the autism community in myriad ways. Dave once stated that his *"peak skill is being able to use words to describe what it is like to have autism."* Dave's gentle and thoughtful manner, articulate explanations, and enlightening visual images make a powerful impact on all who hear him speak.

Dave's contributions touch people locally, nationally, and internationally. He participates on panels of adolescents and adults with high functioning autism at our Asheville TEACCH teacher trainings. Dave has presented at professional events such as TEACCH Winter Inservice and the *1998 Swedish Autism Society Asperger Syndrome Conference*, near Stockholm. One of his essays has been published in *High Functioning Autism or Asperger Syndrome?* in the series *Current Issues in Autism*, edited by Eric Schopler, Gary Mesibov, and Linda Kunce.

Dave attends *Autreat*, an annual retreat sponsored by Autism Network International (ANI), an organization by and for people with autism. *(See Recommended Resources.)* One year Dave and his wife taught a workshop at Autreat on relationships. Last year Dave gave a presentation titled *Practical Autism* which focused on ways to use one's talents in everyday life.

Dave also serves on the Asheville TEACCH Center Parent Advisory Board, as well as on the Enrichment Training Center Board. He is a community representative to the Board of the Autism Society of North Carolina. A typical day is structured around his activity on the Internet. To read some of Dave's essays, poems, and presentations, go to **http://webpages.charter.net/dspicer**

Dave is a fascinating client, a well-respected and admired colleague, and best of all, a good friend.

Irene Vassos

Irene Vassos is a talented fabric artist, delightful musician and singer, and gifted Technology Coordinator for Pittsfield Public Schoools in the Berkshire Mountains of western Massachusetts. She is particularly inspired when creating databases and training people to use her beloved Macintoshes in creative ways. One of her many extensive projects was to design a database that is used for her school system's special education department. With the proceeds from the sale of this database, Irene is promoting the establishment of an educational foundation to fund autism training for teachers in her area.

Irene's encouragement and computer consultation helped keep me on track from the very beginning to the end of this book. She breathes life into her many creative projects, and I was fortunate to have Irene's help with this one. Her computer skills and eye for design are at the core of this book's visual appeal.

The best thing about Irene is that she is my cousin.

Recommended Resources

This is an alphabetical listing of the resources mentioned in this book, as well as the author's most frequent recommendations to teachers, therapists, and parents. Books can be ordered through from *Future Horizons* and the *Autism Society of North Carolina Bookstore.*

Asperger's Syndrome: A Guide for Parents and Professionals
by Tony Attwood
An excellent overall book for teachers, parents,... everyone! Very readable and complete! Check out Tony's web site at **www.TonyAttwood.com**

Asperger Syndrome: A Practical Guide for Teachers
by Val Cumine, Julia Leach, and Gill Stevenson
Full of teaching strategies, especially great for teachers.

Asperger Syndrome and Difficult Moments
by Brenda Smith Myles and Jack Southwick
The "big picture" in understanding and preventing behavior problems when the child has Asperger Syndrome or high functioning autism.

Albert Einstein
by Ibi Lepsky and Paolo Cardoni
A charming children's book about "...a child different from all others." No mention is made about autism or Asperger Syndrome, but one cannot help but wonder... Useful to read to children when helping them understand their peer who has AS or HFA. Can be used in conjuction with *Understanding Friends* and *The Sixth Sense. (See Chapter 9)*

Autism Network International (ANI)
ANI is an autistic-run self-help and advocacy organization for autistic people. Contact information:

Autism Network International (ANI)
P.O. Box 448
Syracuse, New York 13210-0448
www.ani.ac

The Autism Society of America

ASA serves the needs of individuals with autism and their families through advocacy, education, public awareness, and research. They hold a conference every summer. For information, call or visit their Web site.

Autism Society of America
7910 Woodmont Ave., Suite 300
Bethesda, MD 20814-3015
www.autism-society.org
800-3-AUTISM ext.150
301-657-0881

The Autism Society of North Carolina (ASNC)

ASNC serves individuals with autism and their families in North Carolina. ASNC provides comprehensive advocacy, information and referral, as well as a spectrum of direct services designed to increase opportunities in employment, housing, skills training, education, parent support, and respite. ASNC also runs two summer camps for adults and children with autism, and assists local parent support groups in the state. ASNC produces a quarterly newsletter, *The Spectrum*, for its members and operates the largest bookstore of titles related to autism in the country. They also run a Resouce Center which offers two-week loans of books and videos, including *Paul at Three*, the video which features Paul Hoyt (one of this book's illustrators) and his family, when Paul was three years old . Write or call:.

Autism Society of North Carolina (ASNC)
505 Oberlin Road, Suite 230
Raleigh, NC 27605-1345
www.autismsociety-nc.org
E-mail: jlawson@autismsociety-nc.org

Comic Strip Conversations

by Carol Gray

Comic Strip Conversations were mentioned in several times in this book. Carol Gray's booklet, published by Future Horizons, gives complete information on developing and using social stories.

Future Horizons

Future Horizons is the largest publisher of books and tapes on autism, and offers conferences across the USA and internationally. For information visit their informative web site, write, or call:

Future Horizons
721 W. Abram St.
Arlington, TX 76013
www.FutureHorizons-autism.com
E-mail: edfuture@onramp.net

Higher Functioning Adolescents and Young Adults with Autism: A Teacher's Guide

by Ann Fullerton, Joyce Stratton, Phyllis Coyne, and Carol Gray
An excellent collection of valuable information and strategies. "A must-read" even if your child has not yet reached adolescence.

High Functioning Autism or Asperger Syndrome?

Edited by Eric Schopler, Gary Mesibov, and Linda Kunce
Each May, TEACCH sponsors a conference in Chapel Hill devoted to a different issue concerning autism. The conference brings national and international experts together for formal presentations and discussions of research, clinical findings, and personal observations. These scholarly volumes in the *Current Issues in Autism Series*, published by Plenum Press, are the result of TEACCH's May conferences. *High-Functioning Autism or Asperger Syndrome?* is the most recent addition to the series. An excerpt by Linda Kunce and Gary Mesibov titled "Educational Approaches to High Functioning Autism and Asperger Syndrome" was included in this book on page 190.

Indiana Resource Center for Autism (IRCA)

The *Nine Types of Lesson Adaptations*, listed in Chapter 9, are representative of the strategies promoted by IRCA for special learners. It was included in this book with the permission of Cathy Pratt. For more information on the Indiana Resource Center for Autism, write or call:

Cathy Pratt, Director
Indiana Resource Center for Autism (IRCA)
Institute for the Study of Developmental Disabilities
2853 E. Tenth Street
Bloomington, IN 47408-2696
www.isdd.indiana.edu/~irca

💻 Jypsy'slink

This Web site's home page claims *"More autism-related links than you can shake a stick at!!!!..."* At the time of this writing, there are 658 links, and more importantly, they are arranged in a user-friendly format. The address is **www.isn.net/~jypsy/autilink.htm**

📖 The MAAP (More Able Autistic People)

This organization, with Susan Moreno at the helm, was among the earliest support devoted specifically to those with high functioning autism. For many years, MAAP has been disseminating information and giving support to families and individuals with HFA, especially notable in the early days when the literature and knowledge was very scarce about HFA. The booklet, **High-Functioning Individuals with Autism: Advice for Parents and Others Who Care,** written by Susan Moreno and edited by Anne Donellan, remains a valuable source of information. It is a small booklet, which makes it easy to share with new teachers and family members. We always keep a healthy stack of these booklets available at our TEACCH Center and give them to parents of newly diagnosed children and adolescents, and to new teachers of students with high functioning autism. As mentioned in Chapter 9, this booklet also contains a description of how to present an "autism sensory stimulation" to a group of students. This informative booklet can be ordered through MAAP, which also publishes a newsletter, and sponsors conferences.

The MAAP
MAAP Services, Inc.
P.O. Box 524
Crown Point, Indiana 46307

📖 Mind Mapping

One of the earliest published sources of this visual strategy can be found in the book, **Use Both Sides of Your Brain,** by Tony Buzan, published in 1974. I learned mind mapping from Robert and Helena Stevens of Mastery Systems, Inc. Variations of *mind mapping* have been referred to as "semantic organizers" or "graphic organizers" and given various names such as *topic mapping, webbing,* and *bubbling.* Besides being featured in this book, other current books suggest this strategy, including two on this recommended recource list: **Higher Functioning Adolescents and Young Adults with Autism,** by Fullerton, et al, and **Asperger Syndrome and Difficult Moments**, by Myles and Southwick.

📖 The Morning News

edited by Carol Gray

The Morning News is an excellent quarterly publication *"dedicated to individuals with autism and those who work alongside them to improve mutual understanding"*. Each issue is full of practical information for parents, teachers, and individuals with autism, as well as containing an extensive pen-pal registry. To subscribe, contact:

The Morning News
Carol Gray, Editor
Jenison High School
2140 Bauer Road
Jenison, Michigan 49428

💻 O.A.S.I.S.
(Online Asperger Syndrome Information and Support)

This Web site was created by Barbara Kirby, a mother of a child diagnosed with Asperger Syndrome. This site is rich with information and links. The O.A.S.I.S. address is **www.udel.edu/bkirby/asperger**.

📖 Pretending to be Normal: Living with Asperger's Syndrome

by Liane Holliday Willey

A personal account, complete with tips and survival skills for adults with AS. She has the diagnosis herself, as does one of her daughters.

📖 A Real Person

by Gunilla Gerland

This personal account has been translated from Swedish. Gunilla gives an articulate account of what life is like with autism from the "inside". Even if you have read many other first-person accounts, you *must* read this one! The author's clarity and honesty brings the reader's understanding of autism to a new level. Each page provides vivid insights for those of us who live with, work with, care about, or are a person with autism.

📖 The Sixth Sense

Mentioned in Chapter 9, the lesson plan for presenting *The Sixth Sense* can be found in the booklet, **Taming the Recess Jungle**, by Carol Gray.

📖 Social Stories

For information about Social Stories see the following resources by Carol Gray:

The Original Social Story Book
The New Social Story Book
Writing Social Stories with Carol Gray *(videotapes and workbook)*

🖥 Dave Spicer

Dave contributed the section for parents and teachers at the end of Chapter 4 about developing your child's artistic talent, and is quoted several times throughout this book. A sampling of his poems and essays, including his presentations on his personal experiences with autism, can be found on his Web site: **http://webpages.charter.net/dspicer**

🖥 TEACCH

North Carolina's program for the *Treatment and Education of Autistic and related Communication handicapped CHildren* **(TEACCH)** is a Division of the Department of Psychiatry of the School of Medicine at the University of North Carolina at Chapel Hill. TEACCH is dedicated to improving the lives of children and adults with autism. It is a comprehensive, community based program that includes direct services, consultation, research, and professional training. TEACCH, founded by Eric Schopler, and directed by Gary Mesibov, is funded by state and federal funds, and by private gifts and memorials. Eight regional TEACCH Centers, and the TEACCH Administrative and Research Center, provide diagnostic evaluations and support for individuals with autism of all ages and their families. TEACCH was the early leader in developing visually structured teaching strategies which have been adopted by programs, worldwide. For information on the TEACCH program, its research activities, or out-of-state training, consulting, and diagnostic services, contact:

Division TEACCH Administration and Research
CB# 7180, 310 Medical School Wing E
The University of North Carolina at Chapel Hill
Chapel Hill, NC 27599-7180

Tel: 919-966-2174
Fax: 919-966-4127
www.teacch.com

*The **Asheville TEACCH Center** is the professional home of the author, illustrators, and local contributors to this book. They can be reached by writing:*

Asheville TEACCH Center
168-B South Liberty Street
Asheville, NC 28801
Tel: 828-251-6319, ext. 16

📖 Teaching Your Child the Language of Social Success,

by Marshall Duke, Stephen Nowicki, Jr., and Elisabeth Martin
Not only does this book cover the subject of body language and other nonverbal communication skills in a very readable manner, but it includes assessment strategies, a multitude of teaching ideas, and an amazing glossary of facial expressions, gestures, and postures. This book was not specifically written to be used with children or adults with HFA or AS, although almost anything one would want to know about body language can be found somewhere in this book. It can be read simply to enlighten, or for teaching ideas to adapt for your child.

📖 There's a Boy in Here

by Judy and Sean Barron
This book contains enlightening accounts by Sean Barron, a young adult with autism who, recalling his childhood, explains in detail why he behaved the way he did. Sean's excerpts are interspersed within his mother's memoirs. Judy Barron struggled with parenting a child with autism at a time when very little was understood about it and there was limited support for families. Even though this book is currently out of print, it is worth the extra effort to locate a copy. It is recommended especially because of Sean's articulate first-person accounts.

📖 Thinking in Pictures – and Other Reports From My Life With Autism

by Temple Grandin
Another classic from Temple Grandin. Her first book, **Emergence: Labelled Autistic,** led the way for first-person accounts by adults with autism. This second book is definitely a must-read!

💻 Understanding Friends:

Mentioned in Chapter 9, *Understanding Friends*, by Catherine Faherty, is helpful in explaining differences, including autism, to groups of children. The basic lesson plan, which is meant to be changed and individualized according to the needs of the class and the peer(s) with autism, can be found on the TEACCH Web site at **www.teacch.com**

The author with some of the illustrators and contributors, from left to right: Paul Hoyt, Catherine Faherty, John Engle, Maria White, Thomas Johnson, and Dave Spicer with his son, Andrew.

October 1999 - Asheville, North Carolina